Is Consulting for You?

A Primer for Information Professionals

Ulla de Stricker

AMERICAN LIBRARY ASSOCIATION

Chicago   2008

Composition by ALA Editions in Minion and Univers typefaces using InDesign 2 on a PC platform.

Printed on 50-pound white offset, a pH-neutral stock, and bound in 10-point cover stock by McNaughton & Gunn.

The paper used in this publication meets the minimum requirements of American National Standard for Information Sciences—Permanence of Paper for Printed Library Materials, ANSI Z39.48-1992. ∞

Library of Congress Cataloging-in-Publication Data

De Stricker, Ulla.
    Is consulting for you? : a primer for information professionals / Ulla de Stricker.
        p.   cm.
    Includes bibliographical references and index.
    ISBN-13: 978-0-8389-0947-8 (alk. paper)
    ISBN-10: 0-8389-0947-7 (alk. paper)
    1. Library consultants—Vocational guidance. 2. Information consultants—Vocational guidance. I. Title.
    Z682.4.C65D4 2008
    023'.2—dc22   2007021921

ISBN-13: 978-0-8389-0947-8
ISBN-10: 0-8389-0947-7

Printed in the United States of America

12   11   10   09   08   5   4   3   2   1

Contents

Preface

Who Should Read This Primer?

This primer is intended as a guide for librarians and for professionals in other information-centric industries *who are considering a move into consulting*. Building on my personal experience and the experience of other consultants, it offers a realistic look at what it's like to earn one's living project to project, client to client—and some tips from real life. As any of my consultant colleagues would tell you, "It is a mistake to think one can be a successful consultant on the strength of one's professional skills. There is a lot more to consulting than most might think."

If you are pondering the possibility of setting up a practice but aren't sure you are ready or have what it takes, part 1 of this book is your point of departure; it suggests key questions you should consider carefully. If you are certain you are going to proceed, you may want to begin your reading in part 2 to get a sense of the practicalities of establishing your business and some pointers regarding the client relationship.

Consulting Opportunities Are Expanding

As the "information sphere" evolves and the library profession continues to undergo change, many librarians are considering career options beyond the environments in which they have typically been active. At the same time, the demographics of the profession have begun to create considerable gaps as retirement culls the ranks of employed librarians. The wave of retirement among librarians could create opportunities for consultants as library managers devise strategies for the future of their libraries—just as newly retired librarians may consider offering their experience on a project basis.

Two factors are increasing interest in consulting as a career move. First, the pace of change in most organizations is so fast that project-by-project management is the norm. To meet marketplace demands, organizations must adapt and develop quickly—which calls for just-in-time expertise. Second, more and more professionals face the simultaneous challenge of raising their own families and caring for aging parents—which calls for flexible work arrangements. Consulting work, with its opportunities for negotiating deliverables and time frames to accommodate many other commitments, is attractive to those who juggle multiple responsibilities.

What Is Library Consulting and What Assignments Do Librarians-Turned-Consultants Undertake?

The expression "library consulting" encompasses two complementary meanings. It denotes librarians who offer their unique skills to a variety of clients, not necessarily in libraries. It also denotes the activity of other types of professionals (e.g., architects, staff training experts) who offer their services to libraries and library-like entities.

Whether you are a library professional or a professional in another discipline, your opportunities will likely appear in the following markets:

Libraries and library-like entities such as archives and records centers. Typically, consultants are called in when a special project requires unique expertise. The design and construction of a new building; the selection and implementation of a library management system, document repository, or enterprise search system; and the development and marketing of new services are examples.

Nonlibrary knowledge-intensive settings. In corporate and government entities focusing on market research and competitive intelligence, customer care, policy development, advocacy, and the like, consultants are typically engaged to create mechanisms for information support of various kinds. Librarians are particularly effective in such consulting roles.

Information and publishing industries. Librarians and information scientists play significant roles in developing, marketing, selling, and supporting a wide range of content-based products and services.

Consulting spans a range from highly specialized, focused activities (e.g., procuring and installing an integrated library system) to broad, strategic efforts (e.g., information services reengineering). An individual consultant's personal preferences—delivering on very specific and concrete assignments versus designing multifaceted solutions where any number of approaches could be considered—are factors in how he or she goes about building the consulting business.

Some consultants decide to focus on one service or market segment (e.g., offering services related to library technology, or services aimed at academic libraries); others offer a variety of services to clients in one or more sectors. As a simple generalization, we might distinguish four consulting scenarios in the "library and information sphere," as follows:

Librarians offering consulting services to libraries and library-like entities	Other professionals offering consulting services to libraries and library-like entities
Librarians offering consulting services to nonlibrary clients	Other professionals offering consulting services in various areas of information and knowledge management to nonlibrary clients

A Note on the Examples

Throughout the text, I have used illustrative scenarios or hypothetical situations as examples to provide clarity. Such illustrations are derived from my own and colleagues' collective and accumulated experience over several decades. While they are representative in a general sense, the illustrations contain elements from multiple events and none point to actual organizations, individuals, or projects.

Acknowledgments

In preparing this primer, I sought help from colleagues who offered their comments on what it's like to be a consultant. As I had hoped they would, they reinforced my own perceptions, allowing me to offer the suggestions made in this primer with confidence.

In addition to expressing my appreciation to friends and colleagues I have had the privilege of working with over the years, I want to give a big thank-you to those who gave generously of their time in interviews: Pat Cavill, Donna Cohen, Davita Crawford, Chris Donohue, Josh Duberman, Shelly Edwards, Ken Haycock, Jill Hurst-Wahl, Sara Laughlin, Sandra Morden, Maria Phipps, John Savage, Denise Shockley, Jan Sykes, and Barbara Wagner.

In addition, I thank my valued colleagues Dr. Paul Nicholls and Stephen Barringer for the research and editorial assistance they graciously gave me.

Part One

Considerations
for Prospective
Consultants

What Is Consulting, Exactly?

I would love to have your opportunities to travel!" "I always dreamed of being able to set my own hours!" "Imagine, no more commuting!"

For those working in full-time jobs, the lifestyle of a consultant may appear to be one of ease and leisure. They may envy the flexibility in scheduling work—for example, the luxury of being able to decide which projects to accept—and the benefits of working from home, to name but a few of the major perceived advantages. Although those advantages most certainly are appealing, there are realities to deal with as well: the tendency for work to be uneven, the challenge of managing expectations within preset budget envelopes, the considerable time and effort going into networking—again, to name just a few.

In this chapter we take a look at the basics: What is consulting—beyond the superficial characteristics of working at home in one's sweats? Why do consultants get hired, and who hires them?

Why Are Consultants Needed?

As individuals, we take for granted the need to seek out and pay for the services of an expert who can help us deal with a specific situation we wouldn't dream of tackling—or couldn't tackle—ourselves. We gladly pay for the services of mechanics. (It is theoretically possible that I could learn to fix my own car when it breaks down, but what would be the sense of investing the time when in all likelihood I would be in need of car repairs only now and then?) Library managers follow the same paradigm when they call on a consultant to help plan the interior of a new library, fashion a communications strategy, select and implement a content management system for the intranet, and the like.

Of course, the practice of purchasing professional assistance when needed goes far beyond such relatively few-and-far-between occasions as outfitting a new library. Most libraries and similar knowledge-based entities (e.g., competitive intelligence units, marketing departments, risk analysis teams) lack the personnel to carry out all the projects that must be undertaken. When a library system must be upgraded; when it's time to market an expanded range of services to existing and new clients; when a body of material needs to be digitized; when libraries in a region need to develop new ways to collaborate—consultants are called in to plan, guide, and assist in processes that do not fall within the day-to-day operations.

Generally, it is understood that the value of a consultant's expertise more than justifies the cost. Here's why:

Engaging consultants makes business sense. Library directors are keenly aware of the benefits resulting from just-in-time procurement of expertise. More important, the variety of business, technical, and strategic challenges facing most libraries and library-like entities is so great that no other option exists but to lean on targeted expertise when special circumstances arise. For example, the development from scratch of a program to support a distance learning initiative could require experience falling outside that of current staff in an academic library.

Consultants bring a fresh perspective. A compelling benefit to engaging the services of consultants is the fact that they are unencumbered by the past. They have no traditions lurking in the backs of their minds as they go about their projects; in fact, it can be a risk for a consultant to become too closely entwined in the client's operations. Conversely, consultants bring along experience from their previous projects in other settings. No amount of benchmarking can match that breadth of experience.

Consultants represent a time-limited commitment for the client. When the consultant's report is in hand, the client is free to consider whether to proceed with the consultant's recommendations. Although all consultants hope their clients implement the recommended approach—immediately—reality says otherwise. Sometimes clients aren't ready for the changes recommended, budget limitations get in the way, or sudden new developments put plans on hold.

Consultants are a solution to a communications challenge. Inasmuch as the "hard truth" can be easier to accept if it comes from an outsider, consultants are sometimes asked to take care of a function that could be difficult for a manager to perform. As a result, consultants may find themselves bearing an uncomfortable message, thus needing considerable finesse in the area of communications.

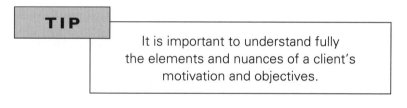

TIP

It is important to understand fully the elements and nuances of a client's motivation and objectives.

Consulting Roles

Consulting activities are extremely varied, yet they share characteristics. In your consulting career, you may get to function in every role from summer relief to miracle worker, and you will intuitively recognize that different work tasks and tangible outputs are appropriate according to the nature of a given project. Assignments can be quite straightforward, as in "Select and install a new library management system"—or more nuanced, as in "Please help us determine how we can best meet the needs of the students in the distance learning program."

For successful outcomes, the roles consultants play must be clearly understood, both by the consultant and by the client. There is trouble ahead if it turns out the client and the consultant have different views of what the consultant should contribute to a given project.

The list below illustrates the range of roles consultants may find themselves performing. Naturally, individual consultants may gravitate to certain types of roles and focus their offerings accordingly.

Example of Consulting Role	*Implications*
An extra pair of hands: A hiring freeze may prevent adding new staff, but a contractor can be engaged.	The consultant works within preexisting guidelines and may have limited opportunity to be creative.

- Fill in for someone on leave.
- Supervise the completion of a cataloging backlog.
- Manage the merger of two libraries or collections.

Special-purpose assistance: No one on staff is available to carry out a special project.

The consultant may work under the direction of a manager on staff and may not have much scope for bringing about significant change.

- Teach staff how to use a new system or tool.
- Prepare a special exhibit.
- Conduct market research: what do current and potential clients need?

Unique expertise: The client needs advice on how to deal with a particular challenge.

In this role, the consultant is sought out specifically to bring to bear expertise that is not already on hand. Typically the consultant conducts a study of "how things are now" and prepares a set of recommendations for concrete actions, designs, purchases, and so forth.

- How can we improve work flow in technical services?
- What are the best options when it comes to staffing up and selecting software for a new intranet?

Example of Consulting Role	Implications

Example of Consulting Role

- How can we make the new library wing blend in with the original building and yet stand out as a strong architectural statement?
- What technology infrastructure will be adequate for current and future needs?

"Been there, done that": The client wants to minimize risk by engaging someone who is very familiar with activities similar to the project at hand.

- How can we figure out what services to prioritize and what services to terminate?
- How can we improve the visibility of the resource center among the market analysts?

Visionary strategist: "Help us chart the way"

- We know we need some kind of knowledge repository for the call center agents, but we have no idea where to begin.
- We need to strengthen our role in, and contribution to, the community we serve; what are the components in meeting such a challenge?

Implications

In many situations, the client is particularly keen on knowing that the consultant has carried out similar projects and therefore can apply proven techniques. If receptivity to new approaches is limited, it is the consultant's challenge to convince the client to try something novel.

This role requires a mix of broad expertise across the gamut of the project's components as well as considerable skills in managing complex projects.

Example of Consulting Role	*Implications*
Agent of change: Organizational and psychological challenges stand in the way of moving forward. ■ Design and lead a series of exercises to help staff arrive at conclusions and insights that will facilitate their acceptance of change. ■ Facilitate exploratory sessions to identify friction points and opportunities.	In some library and library-like settings, strong traditions exist for how things are done, and it can be difficult for the current director to get staff members excited about new priorities, services, or processes. In such a case, the consultant's role is to facilitate changes in employee attitudes.
Rescuer: Specific events require specialized expertise. ■ A fire has caused sprinkler damage to irreplaceable materials. Now what? ■ Several of the senior staff have taken early retirement, and a sudden illness has left a significant gap in staffing. How can we get through the next few months, and how do we deal with the planning for human resources?	Though it would be nice if skills such as salvaging wet books were not needed, the fact is that accidents do happen, and consultants who know what to do are needed—now. The best laid plans of library directors can't prevent a staffing crisis; it is fortunate that some consultants specialize in dealing with such situations.

What Roles Appeal to You?

The variety of consulting roles offers opportunities for everyone willing to deal with the realities we touch on in chapter 3. Those pondering a consulting career move may wish to reflect on their personal work styles and consider questions such as these:

Am I at ease in situations where the "sky's the limit except for the budget" and creativity is wanted—meaning I may have to step outside my official areas of expertise?

Do I prefer projects that are clearly focused on work flow, operational processes, and technology?

Do I have what it takes to deal with and resolve conflicting stakeholder priorities (a.k.a. politics)?

Would I prefer to "get down and dirty with the boxes" during a short, intensive project yielding visible results quickly—or to work away slowly at an opinion-shaping communications effort that could take two years and whose impact it would be difficult to prove?

Freelancing Is Not the Same as Consulting

Consulting is a subtle business. You come into an organization as an outsider and bring your professional experience to bear on guiding the client and recommending what in your judgment is the best course of action, given the situation at hand.

In the list above, the first two roles represent situations I would characterize as freelancing rather than consulting. Widely used in the information technology community, freelancers or "outsourced personnel" keep the operations of many organizations humming.

No value judgment is implied in the distinction, and all the benefits and challenges mentioned in chapters 2 and 3 apply equally to consultants and freelancers. One important difference should, however, be noted: if freelance work entails well-defined activities and deliverables, the freelancer may enjoy a high level of comfort that "I know precisely what I am doing"; in more fluid consulting assignments where many options are possible, it may be more difficult to feel quite so confident.

Who Hires Consultants?

It is a potential obstacle for consultants that the hiring process may be complex. A middle manager may, for example, need to execute quite an elaborate business case and "sales job" to obtain senior management approval for the budget to hire a consultant. That said, there are some markets in which the decision to engage a consultant or consulting firm is a foregone conclusion (e.g., we need to build a new library), and work proceeds immediately to produce a Request for Proposal (RFP) or similar instrument for attracting candidates.

Naturally, the size of a consulting contract has a bearing on who in an organization has the ability to engage consultants. Small discretionary budget envelopes for "special projects" are not uncommon, and many consultants enjoy the ease with which engagements come about in such cases. Those bidding for very large projects are familiar with the longer time frames involved when top executives are deciding which consulting firm to engage.

As in every sales context, the key is reaching the decision maker. He or she may or may not sit in the audience when a consultant delivers a speech at a library conference.

The Outlook

Is Consulting a Viable Option for Librarians? Is the Library Market Viable for Other Types of Consultants?

Naturally, any information professional contemplating consulting will have scoured the Internet to identify (1) "who else is doing what I want to do" and (2) "where my potential clients congregate on the Internet."

Established library consulting firms and individuals marketing their library-related services can be identified readily on the Internet. They help libraries deal with all aspects of their operations, as outlined below. In addition, some state libraries employ consultants who assist public libraries according to state policy; researching the consulting offerings of state libraries could be a good starting point for pinpointing the needs of the public library community in your region.

Typical Areas of Consulting Activity

Every aspect of library and library-related operations represents an opportunity for consultants to offer their expertise to clients in need of project support. The following is intended as a brief overview of the types of activities consultants in the library sphere undertake.

SERVICES OFFERED TO LIBRARIES

Facilities

Library facility planning, construction, expansion, reconstruction, and restoration. Projects focus on library space and service needs assessments, interior space planning and design, architectural plan reviews, and related services.

Organizational Infrastructure

Needs assessment, policy development, planning, evaluation, selection, implementation, documentation, and staff training associated with library infrastructure systems spanning a broad range:

- Integrated library management systems
- Internet and intranet functions
- Wireless access
- Public access Internet stations

Content and Collections

Assistance with typical and familiar library functions, whether as a generalist or a specialist in library skills or a given subject. Content and collections encompass many media and formats, each posing particular storage and access requirements. Projects include

- Creation of needs-based collection development policies
- Product and vendor research
- Procurement and vendor relations management
- Classification, taxonomies, indexing, cataloging, metatagging
- Weeding, archiving, off-site storage
- Preservation and restoration

Operations

Planning, details, and management of day-to-day library procedures and functions. Specific tasks may range from policy development, research, evaluation, planning, and implementation of a security or sprinkler system to management of a cataloging department during a regular staffer's maternity leave. Typical projects may include

- Service management
- Security (safety of persons)
- Protection (theft prevention)
- Facilities maintenance

Human Resources

All aspects of the library's human resource management, including in-house training programs and development of associated printed and electronic materials. Typical projects may include

- Skills requirement identification and recruiting
- Orientation and task-specific training
- Ongoing professional development
- Resolution of staff relations challenges

Stakeholder Needs-Based Service Development

Determining and effectively servicing the needs of the various library stakeholder groups. Typical projects may include

- Research into client needs and "information preferences"
- Strategic plan development
- Business plan development
- Policy development

Library Services to Special Groups

Specialized aspects of any library service as they relate to specific user groups, such as

- Children, young adults
- Minorities
- Visually impaired
- Linguistic groups

Governance, Library Boards, Stakeholder Relations

Maintaining a smooth, informed, and effective relationship with the library's various stakeholder groups, particularly those in governance roles. In the case of public libraries, city councils and regional consortia are important partners. Typical projects may deal with

- Board/trustee relations
- Advisory groups
- User interest groups
- Associated communications tasks

Public Relations and Marketing Library Services

Setting up mechanisms for an effective relationship with the library's stakeholders. Justifying the library's value to budget authorities and similar activity can be involved in addition to traditional public relations to direct library users and the wider community group. Typical projects may include those involved with

- Publicity and advertising
- Press relations and media releases
- Marketing plans, campaigns, and events
- Communications to stakeholders and the public

Compliance

Assistance with the increasingly complex issues surrounding compliance with the law. Projects may involve

- Building and safety codes
- Access for the disabled
- Privacy
- Pornography and hate crime

Market Research

Planning, execution, analysis, and presentation of virtually any type of research program the organization may require. Projects may be straight-forward or complex, involving extensive surveys requiring a detailed research plan, multiple data collection instruments, sophisticated statistical analysis, and detailed reporting. Typical projects may require

- Any kind of research needed internally for planning—what other libraries are doing

- Survey process needed to determine client needs
- Measures of the effectiveness of current services
- Forecasts based on demographic and economic trends

Grant Writing

Assistance in the tasks associated with identifying, applying for, and obtaining external funding for programs or initiatives. A dedicated effort is often required for success, and grantsmanship is a specialized skill. Using a consultant can be a cost-effective investment. Typical projects include

- Research to identify available funding sources
- Research to identify information required by the granting entity
- Organization of the required information
- Preparation of the application and associated backup material

SERVICES OFFERED TO NONLIBRARY ENTITIES
(e.g., publishers, software/systems companies)

Strategic Planning
- Assistance in determining business and market strategy

Product (Re)development and Design
- Design of interfaces and functionality
- Management of beta/usability testing
- Ongoing solicitation and interpretation of user feedback

Market Research/User Requirements Assessments
- Competitive intelligence—what the competitors are offering
- What librarians are saying they want the vendor community to offer

Customer Service
- Assessments of the "user experience" and the implications for client service and training

Training

■ Development of training and help materials, workshops, and on-demand tutoring tools

Identifying Consultants

Personal referrals are the number-one method by which consultants and clients find each other. That said, some specialized finding tools are available:

ALA's Library Administration and Management Association (www.ala.org/lama/lama.htm) publishes *Library Consultants Directory,* an annual feature of its *Library Administration and Management* magazine.

As well, ALA's *American Libraries* features consultancies both in print and online in ConsultantBase. The *Library Building Consultants List* (https://cs.ala.org/lbcl/search/) is a good starting point for libraries, administrators, and architects who want to employ a library consultant.

Similarly, the Special Libraries Association (SLA) Consultation Services Committee developed the CONSULT Online (www.sla.org/consultonline/) directory of SLA members who are library consultants.

An independent finding tool is Library Consultants Directory Online (www.libraryconsultants.org), which lists a limited number of consultants by name, expertise, or state.

State libraries typically offer the services of consultants on staff or can make referrals.

National, regional, state, and local library associations are excellent as sources of pointers to potential consultants.

Specialized library associations (e.g., American Association of Law Libraries) are often the best places to go when it comes to finding experts focused on a given type of library or operational area.

Presentations given by consultants at conferences offer a preview of their competencies.

Of course, you could hire a consultant to first prepare your RFP and then find, evaluate, and hire another consultant.

Opportunities within the Library Community

The current climate of downsizing and a graying workforce (Stevens 2005) promises to offer new opportunities for consultants for decades to come. Of the key drivers, three are particularly relevant for library consultants:

- Evolving demographics
- Information technology developments
- Evolution of what libraries—and librarians—actually do

DEMOGRAPHICS: WILL RETIREMENT TRANSLATE INTO AN INCREASE IN CONSULTING PROJECTS?

The Bureau of Labor Statistics placed librarians seventh among occupations with the highest percentage of workers age 45 years and older in 1998 and estimated that 46.4 percent of librarians would leave the workforce during the period 1998–2008. It would be natural to expect our library schools to produce the replacements for the many thousands of retiring librarians. However, annual statistics collected by ALA's Office of Accreditation show that both enrollments and number of faculty remain stable; in other words, it does not appear that the library profession is attracting significantly greater numbers.

Such demographic trends prompted the 2004 Institute of Museum and Library Services initiative to recruit and educate new librarians (funded to the tune of $14.7 million) and a 2005 award (almost $1 million) to the University of North Carolina at Chapel Hill for a national research study on the future of librarians in the workforce (see http://libraryworkforce .org/tiki-index.php). Nevertheless, it will take time to correct a situation that has developed over decades.

Although a graying profession might suggest a bonanza for scarce new graduates, Rachel Singer Gordon advises librarians to "heed the facts. . . . before visions of jobs and promotions dance in our heads, let's look at some more data." She goes on to point out that quite a few librarians may in fact work past age 65, and that those retiring are leaving management positions that may not be filled, and certainly not by recent graduates (Gordon 2004).

In the face of such statistics, would-be library consultants could do well to look at the demographic developments in the regions and niches they consider to be their markets. One analogy worthy of consideration is the pattern seen in large technology firms whose ventures into downsizing led to rehiring former staff as contractors. Yet it cannot be assumed that libraries will hire consultants to pick up the work formerly done by retired staff.

The bottom line is that the information and knowledge management arena is so dynamic and evolves so quickly that predictions would be foolhardy. What we do know is that there is an increasing management awareness of the cost of not dealing appropriately with information challenges. That awareness is our consulting opportunity because we library and information science professionals can help address any such challenge.

INFORMATION AND KNOWLEDGE MANAGEMENT IS THE DOMAIN OF LIBRARIANS

The future of libraries and librarians has been the subject of a great deal of speculation, mostly resulting from the tremendous technological change over the past few decades. Yet there is a general sense that librarians will continue to be needed, albeit with new functions and roles to play for their respective communities and stakeholder groups.

The "now that we have the Internet, we won't need librarians" scenario did not come to pass. On the contrary, many organizations are realizing the value librarians can bring to every aspect of their knowledge-based operations. They put librarians to work in their intranet shops, records management departments, competitive intelligence units, patent offices, customer call centers, information support and data mining operations, and client relations management teams—because librarians have the appropriate information and knowledge management skills.

By keeping an ear to the ground and monitoring trends, consultants can often identify developing demand for new or specialized types of services. Consider the hot areas emerging after 2000—social networking tools, virtual worlds, communities of practice, to name but a few. Special skills in emerging areas can represent a significant advantage for library consultants. At the same time, we must avoid focusing exclusively on too narrow a range, for the relentless pace of change will continually require us to learn new skills.

OPPORTUNITIES OUTSIDE THE CORE
LIBRARY COMMUNITY

Wander into any conference dealing with information technology, and you will see a crowd of professionals struggling with challenges connected to managing information and intellectual capital. Every organization must find ways to find, procure, share, apply, and store information in cost-effective ways, and the principles we have used in managing, say, library content are valid as well in records centers, call centers, sales and marketing departments, laboratories, legal counsel's offices, HR departments—no organization is without some issue tied to information. The trick is finding the precise match between our particular skills and the need for those skills "out there."

One key step in finding that match may well be an exercise in generalizing from the specific library setting to generic organizational settings. Cataloging skills—the art of classifying and describing objects according to a set of rules—can be "mapped out" to inventories of many kinds (think works of art, products in a mail order catalog, work flow procedures, and customer interactions); skills in planning and managing public library programs can be "mapped out" to any type of event management; and so on.

> **TIP**
>
> As an experiment, try describing your own specific expertise without any of the standard library vocabulary.

Scoping Your Own Opportunity

It would be comforting if I could prescribe a list of research steps that would reveal the scope of opportunity for a would-be consultant in a geographic area or particular discipline. Unfortunately, that is impossible. Nevertheless, an enterprising individual curious about the possibilities can consider a research project to assess the outlook in a given professional field and sector. Logical steps would include activities like these, for example:

Assembling and assessing business statistics, economic indicators, and employment trends.

Reading the most recent twelve to eighteen issues of trade or professional journals to determine what subjects are being discussed.

Monitoring the online discussion groups and blogs populated by relevant future colleagues to get a sense of their day-to-day concerns (e.g., the Association of Independent Information Professionals would be appropriate if you intend to go into freelance research).

Once you are familiar with the topics being discussed in certain professional communities, you may want to go further and look into specific conditions that could be indicators of opportunity. Here are a few illustrations:

Someone who has recently completed a records management certificate could pose the following questions about a region or state (some may be fairly easy to answer; others would require quite a bit of digging or estimation based on circumstantial evidence):

- How many certified records managers are graduating from the certificate programs?
- How many records managers are currently employed?
- Are records management positions being advertised?
- Have there been stories in the local press about records management challenges and solutions?
- Are local companies struggling to meet records-related regulations?
- How are businesses going about retaining the incredible volumes of e-mail, never mind searching through the archives for e-mail with particular content?

- How many organizations in the area fall into certain categories and are larger than a certain threshold size, suggesting that they could have records management challenges?

Someone with expertise in developing strategic plans for public libraries could pose these questions about a geographic area:

- What are the business and demographic trends in the urban, suburban, and rural communities?

- What are the plans for new services to be offered by existing public libraries?

- How are library managers currently doing their strategic and operational plans?

- What challenges are being discussed when library managers get together?

A web services specialist might assess the potential for assignments by asking questions such as these:

- How many businesses would fall into a category in which I have specific experience (e.g., small specialty web stores)?

- Could I offer "turnkey" services (e.g., to local clubs, sports leagues, or community organizations whose current web presence is not up to snuff)?

- What could I learn from checking out the websites of organizations listed in various directories (other than concluding that those websites are in need of help)?

Still, when all that is done, there remains one question anyone contemplating consulting should ask: where can I find individuals already working as consultants in my field so that I might set up interviews?

In order to discern the topics currently occupying existing consultants—and by extension their clients—prospective consultants would find it worthwhile to check out the websites of information management–related associations such as these:

Special Libraries Association: www.sla.org

Association of Independent Information Providers: www.aiip.org

AIIM: The ECM (Enterprise Content Management) Association: www.aiim.org

Background Reading

The following list is intended as a starting point for those wishing to dig deeper into the current career outlook in the library sphere. Any librarian will readily be able to identify many more resources.

Abell, Angela, et al. 2006. Roles in the e-landscape: Who is managing information? *Business Information Review* 23 (4): 241–51. http://bir.sagepub .com/cgi/content/abstract/23/4/241.

Australian Library and Information Association. 2005. A worldwide shortage of librarians. Kingston, Australia: ALIA. http://alia.org.au/media.room/ 2005.10.18.html.

Bates, Mary Ellen. 2003. *Building and running a successful research business: A guide for the independent information professional.* Medford, N.J.: Information Today.

Block, Marylaine. 2004. My life as a librarian without walls. *Ex Libris* 233 (November 12). http://marylaine.com/exlibris/xlib233.html.

Careers-in-Business. 2005. Consulting: Facts and trends. http://www.careers-in-business.com/consulting/mcfacts.htm.

Carvell, Linda P. 2005. *Career opportunities in library and information science.* New York: Ferguson.

Cohn, John M., and Anne L. Kelsey. 2005. *Staffing the modern library: A how-to-do-it manual.* New York: Neal-Schuman.

Dority, G. Kim. 2006. *Rethinking information work: A career guide for librarians and other information professionals.* Westport, Conn.: Libraries Unlimited.

Goben, Abigail. 2006. Publishing: A tale of library skills. *Info Career Trends* (September). http://www.lisjobs.com/newsletter/archives/sept06agoben .htm.

Gordon, Rachel Singer. 2004. Get over the "graying" profession hype. *Library Journal* (January 15). http://www.libraryjournal.com/article/CA371074 .html.

———. 2006. *The NextGen librarian's survival guide.* Medford, N.J.: Information Today, Inc.

Heye, Dennie. 2006. *Characteristics of the successful twenty-first century information professional.* Oxford, U.K.: Chandos.

Institute of Museum and Library Services. 2006. Study overview: Future of librarians in the workplace. http://libraryworkforce.org/tiki-index.php; and see the related links.

Karoly, Lynn A., and Constantijn W. A. Panis. 2004. *The 21st century at work: Forces shaping the future workforce and workplace in the United States.* Santa Monica, Calif.: RAND Corporation. http://www.rand.org/pubs/monographs/2004/RAND_MG164.pdf.

Matthews, Brian S. 2006. Librarian as entrepreneur: A blueprint for transforming our future. *Info Career Trends* (November). http://www.lisjobs.com/newsletter/archives/nov06bmathews.htm.

Pemberton, J. Michael, et al. 2006. Creating your career: Minding the gap. *Info Career Trends* (July). http://www.lisjobs.com/newsletter/archives/jul06pemberton.htm.

Plunkett's Consulting Industry. Various consulting industry statistical packages. Houston, Tex.: Plunkett Research. http://www.plunkettresearch.com/Industries/Consulting/tabid/153/Default.aspx.

Sabroski, Suzanne. 2003. Super searchers make it on their own: Top independent information professionals share their secrets for starting and running a research business. Medford, N.J.: Information Today.

Schontz, Priscilla K. 2004. *The librarian's career guidebook.* Lanham, Md.: Scarecrow Press.

SLA Special Libraries Association. 2007. 2006 SLA salary survey and workplace study. Washington, D.C.: Special Libraries Association. Updated annually.

Stevens, Laura. 2005. Where the jobs are: Librarians break into strategic roles. *Wall Street Journal,* April 20. http://www.careerjournal.com/salaryhiring/industries/librarians/20050420-stevens.html.

Webb, Jela. 2005. Setting up as an independent consultant. *FreePint Newsletter* 16 (6). http://www.freepint.com/issues/160605.htm#feature.

3

The Realities of Life as a Consultant

As with most other areas of life, consulting has both an upside and a downside. I review the positive aspects of self-employment in this chapter, along with some realities that should be kept in mind by anyone contemplating the move.

Consulting Is Attractive Because . . .

It is important to be realistic when lining up your reasons for wanting to set up a consultancy. Identifying what benefits and rewards mean most to you will help you cope more easily and feel less disappointed or stressed when challenges do arise. Never underestimate the value of talking things over with a trusted colleague who understands your profession. Independent consulting is a career with unique benefits and frustrations; it is not an easy refuge from an undesirable job situation.

Let's consider the popularly imagined—and sometimes real—attractions of being a consultant. Then, we can look at some associated realities.

I MAKE A DIFFERENCE

In assignments where the client needs holistic help, there is a special reward in being able to say, "I came, I studied, I came up with a solution." Clients' gratitude is a powerful motivator to keep going in our business: "We are so pleased with the system you selected." "Your recommendations for the strategic direction were right on." "We are relieved we could address the issue you flagged before it got too serious." "Soon after we rolled out the new intranet with your recommended marketing, we had tremendously positive feedback from the key groups." And so on.

A special source of satisfaction is the knowledge that we helped instill new skills in others. Sure, as a consultant you can perform an assignment as directed, but it is an added pleasure to know your skills were passed on so that the client staff are in a position to do things they could not do before you got there.

MY EXPERIENCE CAN BENEFIT MANY

Typically, employees do not get to spend most of their time applying core skills; the very operation of an organization demands time for meetings, administrative paperwork, and the like. Consultants have an opportunity to concentrate on activities in *their* area of expertise—which is likely to make them say, "I love what I do."

Taking on an assignment for a client provides a focus—much in the way we expect there to be a focus for an architect we hire to design a house or for the person we call in to dry up a flooded basement. As consultants, we can direct our experience closely at the client's overall or specific challenge—and achieve noticeable results quickly. Thus we can deliver beneficial results, not just to one employer, but to several clients in a given period of time.

Once completed, assignments give consultants a sense of pride: Look at what we accomplished together! Consultants get to have a sense of successful closure more often than some employees do. But they pay for that in subtle ways, as we shall see.

I GET TO KEEP MY SANITY

"I can't take the personality conflicts and the office intrigue." "The endless meetings with no noticeable results are driving me crazy." Most consultants avoid such common employee aggravations, though they face other challenges unique to consulting.

I CAN CHOOSE MY PROJECTS

Very successful consultants do indeed get to choose their assignments and clients because demand exceeds the time available. But many consultants probably accept the majority of engagements offered because there are bills to pay. Still, a consultant has to decide: Even though I am busy, should I take on this project because it will enhance my career? Am I inclined to accept this project because I need the money?

Newly established consultants may feel they ought to build their practices by taking on as much work as they can manage. The risk here is that overcommitting could have adverse consequences.

I'M AT HOME

Working from home is a likely start. The expense of a rented office is not warranted when there is no way to predict income, and in a business where clients rarely need to see our "digs" it makes sense to build a business from a home office. Naturally, working at home brings numerous advantages; being able to look after a family is just one.

I'M IN CHARGE OF MY OWN SCHEDULE

"Not having to race out the door in the morning is a blessing! In fact, I get a lot done as I'm having my morning coffee." "My stress level is way down now that I'm not fighting rush hour traffic every day." "I work harder than I ever have—but I love the flexibility." In today's fast-paced life, the ability to fit appointments, shopping, and chores comfortably into the schedule is understandably appreciated. "I don't mind working late at night when I know I have a free morning the next day to take care of errands."

YOUR REASONS

You are reading this because you are considering the possibility of becoming a consultant. What are your personal motivations? Listing the circumstances and drivers that make you consider the move is a good way to structure your thinking and your discussions with family if you have one:

Are there home life concerns or enablers?

- I can bring up my young children at home while still earning money.
- My teenagers need me, and I can still keep my sanity by working on projects.
- My income is not a crucial factor in paying the mortgage; there is leeway while I build a business.
- As an empty-nester, I have the freedom to focus on my consultancy.
- My aging parents need a fair amount of attention, and I can assist them more easily in a flexible work environment.

Do you want a change in lifestyle?

- Office life is too stressful.
- I have the opportunity to retire early with a package, but I'm not ready to stop working altogether.
- My spouse has retired and we want to be able to travel quite a bit.

Are there extrinsic drivers?

- In the upcoming merger, my job may be eliminated.
- We are moving to another part of the country; it's an opportunity to do something new.

Consulting Is Challenging Because ...

When considering any dramatic career move, it is essential to seek out the experience of those who have gone before. In so doing, you can learn much, and it is a wise investment to spend time with established consultants when planning to enter their ranks. Keeping in mind that those already active as consultants could be concerned about new competitors joining the field, and with due regard for the generosity of future colleagues who take the time and trouble to be your consultant in the consideration phase, explore some of these topics with those who have been there:

- What made you take the plunge? How did you feel about it?
- How did you prepare?

- Where and how did you connect with your first clients?
- How did you go about crafting proposals, deciding what to charge, and otherwise scoping your offering to the clients?
- Were there surprises along the way?
- In retrospect, would you do some things differently?
- What advice would you give those considering becoming consultants?

The following brief overview outlines some key themes in the answers you may hear. Note that these themes pertain to just about any kind of consulting and are not specific to library consulting per se.

I CAN'T PREDICT MY INCOME

In today's economy, job security is a fond memory. But for many, holding a job and having reasonable prospects of earning predictable income for several years beat the need to sell oneself every month. Seasoned consultants may be less concerned because their long track record and reputation generate a consistent stream of inquiries from potential clients. Newer consultants must deal with the fact that, for some years at least, a steady income cannot be taken for granted.

From a financial perspective, setting up a consulting practice is similar to establishing any kind of business—except that you are unlikely to be sitting in front of a banker, presenting a business case for a startup loan to finance manufacturing or service facilities. There is no inventory to buy; the goods to be sold are in your head. But the need for financial resources is there nevertheless. Naturally, personal circumstances are different in every case, and there are no standard rules to go by other than the guidelines dictated by your level of confidence and comfort with risk.

One contract position, then another, and another can gradually evolve into full-time consulting, but such a smooth transition will not happen for everyone. Having sufficient financial resources to meet your obligations even if you make no money for a year or more may be as good a yardstick as any. Unless there is a long lineup of eager clients waiting to be served, it would be risky to assume up front that income is going to flow immediately and steadily thereafter in the first few years. The advice of a financial planner should be sought in any case, since you must understand fully the tax implications of self-employment.

If you are not single, your spouse must be assured that your family's financial resources can handle periods of low income. Be sure to work out a "plan B" together. If you do not have your spouse's wholehearted support for going ahead with setting up a consultancy, you could be adding to your stress level.

SCHEDULES ARE UNEVEN

Most consultants working alone or in small teams will point to the challenge associated with the vagaries of project timing: one quarter they are run off their feet; the next the clients are considering their options. Fiscal year end sometimes drives a flurry of activity when clients decide they do not wish to forfeit budgeted funds; consultants serving the public sector have experience with this feature of scheduling.

For many consultants, a strong network of potential subcontractors is essential for meeting peak demands. Conversely, subcontractors may make themselves available to colleagues whose peak business periods are different from their own.

Seasoned consultants offer a key piece of advice: do not accept projects if you cannot deliver them. Every new contract is welcome, but terrible stress can result if you take on more than you can handle. Experience tells consultants that it is better to say "I am not available until June" than to agree to an April delivery that causes personal havoc. In fact, we know that, generally, clients are willing to wait a month or two (because their own time line estimates may have been overoptimistic too).

TIP

I have worked several months at a stretch without a single day off when the projects piled up. Could you?

SOME PROJECTS ARE QUITE STRESSFUL

Though I have been fortunate and look back on many enjoyable projects, it is realistic to expect that some assignments will be challenging for reasons that are neither professional nor technical. Sometimes you know right away that an assignment could be stressful—for example, potential clients come back to you several times with a request for proposal revisions, are unavailable because of travel, or are late in supplying promised documentation. On the other hand, dealing successfully with the challenges of a "difficult" assignment is a professional learning experience that could be valuable later on.

THERE IS AN IMPACT ON FAMILY LIFE

If you aren't single, your move into consulting may have quite an impact on those closest to you. Your irregular work hours, travels, and unpredictable income can be sources of friction. It is important to prepare family members for the changes associated with the new venture.

More important, your family members may have trouble recognizing that you are "at work" when you are at home; they may find it difficult at first to leave you in peace. A home office with a door to close could be all that is needed, but experience suggests it may take a while before all members of the family really understand that you are not, in fact, at home in the traditional sense while your office door is closed. As a down-to-earth example, you may want to find ways to ensure that typical domestic noises emanating from pets or children do not become apparent to clients on the phone.

Single consultants have the luxury of working all hours without affecting anyone else's schedule. In fact, they often do work all hours, as they choose, for example, to craft reports at night when they are not meeting clients or taking care of daytime errands.

WORK IS ALL AROUND ME

When work is within a few feet of you every minute of every day, you may find it difficult to put it aside, and its physical proximity may make it harder for you to experience true leisure. Salaried employees tend to consider their homes to be their sanctuaries; home-based consultants may want to get out of the house in order to relax. That said, consultants who spend a lot of time on client premises often comment what a luxury it is to "not have to go anywhere this week."

I'M ISOLATED

Unless you work for an established library consulting firm (and there are not many of those) or spend most of your project time on the client's premises, you are likely to be working alone. For some, that is a significant challenge. Some consultants comment on their surprise in discovering just how difficult it is to work in isolation. Not being in an office provides a great deal of freedom—sure we can watch a favorite show in the afternoon if we like—but being outside a standard workplace requires discipline and focus.

Quite a few consultants are so wrapped up in their projects that they can't wait to hit the desk in the morning and in fact spend much more than a typical workday "at work." Others find it is possible to generate the necessary income without working flat out. Regardless of personal style and preferences in terms of scheduling work hours, strong planning skills are a plus—especially if several projects are under way at the same time.

Staying connected professionally is less of an issue today than it might have been in the past, thanks to e-mail, blogs, and the like. Being active in relevant professional associations is a good way to replace the missing office conversations with a reasonable level of social interaction.

TIP

Don't relegate yourself to a cramped corner of your residence. You are going to spend a *lot* of time in your home office—so make it pleasant.

A basement is not recommended unless there is a walkout—you need fresh air and natural light. A spacious bedroom could be a good option if you need to be able to close your door.

Spend the necessary money for a large office desk and cabinetry with plenty of storage so that you can maintain a tidy environment. You want to feel good being in your office.

And don't forget plants and art. An office does not need to be sterile.

Personal Characteristics

Is Consulting a Good Fit?

When librarian consultants discuss among themselves the key reasons they are successful, they often focus on a set of personal characteristics that enable them to tackle the challenges associated with project work and deliver the results clients want. Key among those characteristics is a rock-solid belief in their own abilities and a capacity to avoid becoming depressed or insecure as a result of any untoward project experience.

Some librarians who have become consultants comment that their motivation was a feeling of being out of place in their jobs. Others point out that, in fact, the strong client and service orientation, work ethic, and people skills typical of librarians are major success factors for a consultant. If you are confident that your personality is well suited for consulting, by all means skip to the next chapter, where we deal with the nitty gritty of determining whether there is a market for our intended services.

On the other hand, stepping back to take a look at what motivates and frustrates you can be helpful, just as it is wise to prepare for the situations you know will generate a feeling of stress. If you haven't already participated in exercises designed to characterize personalities, you may want to invest in reading up or getting a professional evaluation. A handy inventory of personality tests can be found at

http://en.wikipedia.org/wiki/Category:Psychological_tests

and several websites provide an opportunity to self-test:

> SimilarMinds.com is a resource for personality tests and personality psychology.

> The Human Metrics Jung Typology Test (www.humanmetrics.com/cgi-win/JTypes2.asp), based on Jung-Myers-Briggs typology, sheds light on your preferences and personality type.

> The Big Five Personality Test (www.outofservice.com/bigfive/) is derived from scientific psychological research, and the feedback provided to participants is based on statistical analyses of large amounts of data.

Crucial Innate Characteristics and Learnable Skills

Academic programs, with good reason, cannot cover in depth the vast array of challenges awaiting graduates in the workplace, much less the situations unique to consulting. Consultants often comment that such difficult-to-nail-down skills as being able to think on their feet, being good at facilitating teamwork, interpreting interpersonal dynamics quickly, and formulating complex subject matter clearly and concisely have been critical success factors for them.

In my own experience, certain personal—as opposed to professional—abilities and skills are vital for maintaining a positive outlook and for staying calm. Again, some general skills are needed by consultants in all industries, but the knowledge-intensive nature of the "library space" and related areas does produce certain characteristic challenges calling for specific strengths. Below, I comment on innate characteristics that would be difficult to learn, and on some skills that can more readily be learned.

The examples I use for illustration are extrapolated from decades of my own experience and the experience of colleagues; they do not point to specific projects or organizations. I stress that each example is but one among many possible ones. The skills I feature are helpful regardless of the size of the project or the fee.

INNATE CHARACTERISTICS

Extreme Patience and Emotional Detachment

The intranet-revamping project seemed straightforward at the beginning. Then some unforeseens turn up: budget cuts eliminate a key resource, and the employee who has been in charge of the project is transferred to another department. In other words, the client's situation is in flux and it is less clear how you, as a consultant, can best be of service now. You are personally keen on the strategy you recommended, but it seems to be unachievable. On top of it all, one staff member believes you aren't necessary—the staff could do the project themselves, without you. Meanwhile, employees in the organization keep complaining about the state of the intranet.

One can lose sleep over less-than-ideal situations. Empathizing with technical services staff who are overwhelmed with the volume of work, agonizing over interpersonal conflicts among staff, chewing over that presentation to management—it's easy to allow client concerns to invade one's consciousness in the middle of the night. Of course, as consultants we must care about our clients, yet we need to keep a professional distance—and we are the more valuable for so doing. We need to realize that things aren't perfect in any organization, and that unless we are specifically hired to address organizational issues we can't deal with them.

Patience is a required attribute. Things do not happen at our pace; legitimate corporate concerns may intervene to delay our projects. What to us looks like a two-week affair could require four approvals from people who may be engaged in higher-priority efforts or may be on vacation. Our direct clients may not have the clout we wish they had in their organizations. We may hand in a brilliant report and ache when we see nothing happening. Time and again I have had to remind myself that, although the report I handed in a week ago looms large for me, it may be but one item on a very long list of matters demanding the client's attention.

Moreover, we need to detach from the outcome of our work. To be sure, we passionately do our best to recommend what should be done. Then we must "get off the project" emotionally, because it is up to the client to proceed. You may find yourself wishing you could hold the client's hand long after the conclusion of a project—but it's unlikely.

As for client staff apprehension about the consultant, consider that to some you are a bright light and to some you are a potential threat. In the latter case, remember that any wariness is not a commentary on your professional qualifications. And hone your trust-building skills!

Questions to ask: Can I get over it if a client does not act on my recommendations? Can I deal with repeated delays and repeated requests for clarification of my proposal without feeling stressed?

Comfort Working Alone: The Buck Stops Here
(if you are a sole or the lead consultant on the project)

In a strategic planning project, you have met with the chief librarian and with all the library staff, individually and in small groups. They have provided their input and viewpoints, even painted scenarios they would love to achieve. You have reviewed the documentation they made available and poked into the work flows and tools they use. Now you are on your own, and you must pull together a coherent presentation of your findings and come up with a set of recommendations the chief librarian can both get buy-in for and implement. There is no one to bounce ideas off, no one to ask for confirmation, no one to encourage you or offer you ideas. It can be very lonely.

Confidence is key. I am happy to carry out solo projects, just as I appreciate the opportunity to assemble a small team.

Engaging other consultants to collaborate on a project can be a wise approach and can be a strong advantage for the client. There are significant benefits in partnering with others, but they are predicated on your absolute trust in the quality of the work the partners produce.

Question to ask: Do I have the experience and courage of conviction to advance a set of recommendations without bouncing them off any-one else?

Ability to Focus, Prioritize, and Schedule:
Time Management

Just as you have created a skeleton document for a project deliverable due next week, the phone rings. A colleague needs, by later today, some estimates for a proposal she is preparing. Three hours from now there's a conference call with members of a committee you are chairing in your professional association, and you haven't had a chance to read the background materials. A check of your e-mail reveals that another client is asking whether you could provide the text for a job posting for a position you recommended adding to the team in a report submitted two weeks ago. The presentation you are giving a month from now is not going to prepare itself. And so on.

The unforeseen and the unpredictable are not unique to consulting, but they are special challenges for consultants—who, naturally, cannot tell their clients that "due to a higher than expected volume of inquiries this month, the report due on August 30 will instead be delivered on September 15." We need to be quite ruthless in determining how to spend each hour of the day. Nice-to-do tasks, such as reviewing resumes for students at the local library school, often end up getting done during what full-time employees consider time off. Our top priority, day in and day out, is the paying client. But can you tell the library school students, "Sorry, I didn't have time for those resumes after all"? Of course not. Everything we have committed to do must be done—dust bunnies or no dust bunnies.

One trick I learned to appreciate is the insertion of uncommitted time, "just in case," into any plans. Something will inevitably spill into such uncommitted time, and knowing I have some maneuvering room reduces stress.

Questions to ask: Can I keep track of the multiple streams of activity in my life? Can I quickly switch gears?

Knack for Absorbing Lots of New Information Quickly and Seeing the Big Picture

The public library must understand the changing demographics of the community and determine how those changes translate into new services. You are called upon to create a service strategy tied to constituent needs. The library's director has amassed a considerable amount of documentation and statistics concerning the demographic, economic, business, and social trends in the community. In order to design the most appropriate series of investigative events, you need to understand what all that information means.

Ingesting and digesting information to draw out the key themes and areas in need of further scrutiny is a special ability that gives a consultant a considerable advantage. It is a success factor for a consultant to be able to spot quickly the meaningful details and distinguish what needs high-priority attention from what can safely be relegated to a lower position on the list of concerns.

Question to ask: Can I get a sense of the main themes in a pile of documents without spending a week reading?

LEARNABLE SKILLS

Communication

In a public sector organization without a library, a relatively new department manager has noted the need for improvements in the practices associated with research and document management. Thanks to a creative response to his RFP for a "Library Study," you won the contract. You soon realize that there are challenges over and above determining what approach to information management would be the most valuable. Why? Because there is wide divergence of opinion in the organization as to the need for "information and knowledge management." It is clear to you that the skepticism about any type of "library" (physical, virtual, professionally staffed or not) stems from several factors often encountered in knowledge-intensive organizations: the subject experts have developed their own ways of dealing with the information they manage and are loath to change their personal habits, much less surrender their files to be managed by someone else. In other words, you have a communication challenge—a selling job—on your hands.

Your interaction with the staff must be extremely nuanced. It would be untoward to imply that highly educated and expert individuals are doing something wrong, but you still need to get to the bottom of how each staff member finds, stores, and later is able (or not) to retrieve various information objects. Therefore, in collaboration with your client, you craft your "message" in such a way as to emphasize that you are there to find ways to save everyone time, relieve stress, and improve productivity. Your message will, no doubt, be adjusted according to the perceptions of staff members; some will welcome the prospect of someone at last doing something; others may be less sure they can see the point of the exercise.

Similarly, when documenting findings, consultants must put their observations carefully. Though the direct client may well agree wholeheartedly with everything we have to say, there can easily be sensitivities on the part of his or her colleagues over what they perceive to be implied criticism.

Question to ask: Do I believe I am able to help others see my vision?

Projection of Authority and Competence

An academic library needs a complete renovation with specific attention to technology needs and the evolving work styles of students (who expect wireless access to everything, a coffee shop, somewhere to stow their backpacks, etc.). In addition, the library wishes to enhance the opportunities for interaction between staff and students, and in general to offer a welcoming and comfortable environment for everyone.

You're on a team of experienced consultants with bold ideas for the renovation. Each of you must instill in the client stakeholder team a sense that "they have come to the right place." You must assure the stakeholders, from the very first moment, that you will deliver a conceptual plan that not only addresses the stated requirements but also brings flair and creativity so that, indeed, the library can become a contemporary academic learning space showcase.

Naturally, we show artists' drawings of our vision and in many other ways substantiate that we understand and creatively approach the elements to be considered in the overall design (e.g., daylight is of short duration for several months in the location in question; noise dampening is a major concern; changing requirements over the longer term indicate a need for movable partitions and walls). But we must also, as individuals, project the kind of authority and competence that will make the client stakeholders feel comfortable entrusting a monumental project to us. How is that done? There is a fine balance between professional certainty ("this is the way to go") and openness to alternatives, and it's a subtle process to manage the confidence of the client as the project evolves from contract negotiations through the delivery phases.

Question to ask: Do I feel, or am I told, that my project expertise, experience, and knowledge come across?

Managing Relationships and Building Rapport and Trust

We consultants need to work hard on our relationships with clients who extend trust in hiring us. Aside from the financial investment, the client must feel comfortable supporting us throughout a project. We want the client to feel proud introducing us to the staff, and we want the client to harvest the accolades when the project succeeds. In addition, we want all staff members to come away with a sense that "that was one fantastic consultant our VP hired."

So here you are, having earned the trust of a client through a high-quality proposal and a convincing initial meeting. As the project gets off the ground, you become aware of strong convictions among staff as to what should be done, and of a lack of enthusiasm on the part of some.

In such a situation (and I stress that they are the exception, yet to be expected at some point in your consulting career), it is wise to spend time on the trust-and-rapport front, as opposed to dealing strictly with the technical matters. Winning over reluctant staff members through relationship management skills is likely the best approach.

What do relationship management skills look like in practice? Only you can tell. My experience is that small gestures such as "Would you have time for a coffee?" can work wonders in providing opportunities for more relaxed conversation so that the consultant and the staff member become human beings with shared concerns. I have found that, once I have had an opportunity to express that "I understand why such a development could be an issue" or "I have seen that difficulty in other settings too," staff members become less anxious.

Questions to ask: Am I secure in dealing with client staff as people? Can I show my own humanity in a dignified way so as to allow them to show theirs?

Negotiation

The RFP mentioned no budget figure. You prepare a proposal showing bronze/silver/gold scopes of effort so that the potential client can consider options. The client reacts positively, indicating (understandably) a desire for the gold option at the bronze or silver price. What to do? You don't want to adopt a take-it-or-leave-it stance (just yet), nor do you want to undercut industry standards.

Perhaps this is a project you don't really need—and given the client's apparent innocence in terms of understanding the scope of the effort, you may hesitate to get involved. But perhaps it is a really interesting assignment, one in which you could bring several associates on board who would be keen and effective.

You get to work creating a new document showing further options, stressing the value of each and pointing out how the client can determine at each phase whether to proceed, thus protecting the option of not committing further funds beyond an initial orientation and some high-level plans for consideration.

The client responds with further communication indicating a reluctance to go beyond a certain investment. At this point, you have drawn on your colleagues' time and spent lots of your own.

In some cases, it is possible to meet with the potential client face to face; in others, it is a matter of a strict exchange of formal documents. In the latter case, I would recommend preparing one last proposal, emphasizing how staff involvement in some tasks could reduce fees. And then I would mentally focus on the belief that I have done my professional best. Should the potential client go with a cheaper offer, you will know that you have probably been spared a stressful project.

In other cases, the potential client may realize that there are more complexities than at first were known. You may then be asked to offer services focused on scoping and defining the project. The end result here could be that, in effect, you end up writing the RFP that will garner the client the best consultants for the job (meaning, possibly, that you are out of the running for the job itself). Ideally, your dealings with the potential client make him or her realize that you are indeed the person to engage, thanks to your in-depth knowledge of the nuances of the challenges at hand.

In chapter 6 we discuss fees. Suffice it to say here that we library consultants owe it to each other to uphold a minimum fee standard—even in a client environment where funding is not typically ample.

Question to ask: Am I able to deal dispassionately with protracted discussions in the phase leading up to an engagement—without getting exasperated?

Business Management and Planning

Even though I am a solo consultant, I am still a business. I become—temporarily—a slightly larger business when I engage two or three subcontractors to assist in a project. I must balance my personal desire to provide the utmost quality for the client at a reasonable fee with the pragmatic need to generate the proper relationship between income and operational costs. Therefore, even though my accountant takes care of the tax returns, I need to have a firm grip on income projections and on the cost of doing business, and I need to be quite savvy when it comes to providing client service at minimum cost to my business. For example, if I'm working on a fixed-price contract, do I take the train or fly to meet the client? What are the business implications for me of the savings from taking the train versus the investment of extra time?

Question to ask: Do I feel secure that I make the best business decisions when it comes to running my practice?

Confidence

I put this skill last because I believe it is a bottom-line requirement for a consultant. However we acquire it, we must possess confidence in our knowledge, experience, and ability to make a difference for our clients. We must exude this confidence in our websites, our public appearances, our professional association work, and our every client interaction, whether written, on the phone, or in person. We must even dress the part.

Question to ask: Am I confident in my skills and my ability to deliver value to clients, and does this confidence come across as genuine?

TIP

Look the part!

I appreciate the fact that my dentist's well-appointed office is in an elegant part of town. I think he's wonderful, and it's comforting to me to see how all his other clients must feel the same way: his success speaks for the quality of his work. I hope my clients get a similar impression from my "consulting uniform"— without thinking, "Oh, so we're funding an opulent lifestyle." I strive for understated, classic elegance and an overall high-quality look to support the message about the work I do.

Characteristics to Be Concerned About

The other side of the above coin is that some characteristics can work against us. It is prudent to be aware if you have any of the following traits:

Procrastination Is Our Enemy

Consultants soon learn that unexpected complexity in a project, or unknown opportunities for enhancements, are common. As a result, projects can "grow" and hence take longer than anyone estimated. It is wise to be ahead of the curve so that there is room for unforeseen events. Just as my aunt lives by the rule that one must always provide time for an unforeseen influenza, so I like to create room for whatever emerges unexpectedly. As an example, if a deliverable is due in two weeks and I'm certain I can produce it in six days, I start now. That way, I accommodate any possible "influenza" that may cause the deliverable to take up more days than anticipated.

Question to ask: Can I justify taking two days off this coming week, knowing I have four days of work to do on my deliverable due next Friday?

Perfection Is Not Always Reasonable

In the real world, good enough sometimes is good enough. Managing any business requires judicious compromises and the ability to see, for example, when doing a particular task will not add materially to the final result. Perfection in a document may not get the client to the next stage of a forward plan.

Question to ask: Is what I am doing a strategic value-added for the client?

Useful Prior Experience

It can be tempting to believe that a set of magic qualities are necessary for success as a consultant—that, somehow, those who have made it possess special qualifications or even special personalities. A corollary belief, then, would be that, "Since I don't have these particular characteristics, I can't make it." The truth—given the sheer number of successful consultants working as we speak—is that everyone has skills, education, and experience applicable to certain types of situations. In knowledge-based jobs, a staff employee is in fact called upon time and again to be a consultant of sorts: leading project teams, dealing with library patrons, negotiating with vendors, and the myriad other tasks we tackled in our "real jobs" all called for creativity, thinking, weighing alternatives, assessing probable outcomes, and plain old sound judgment. Just as it is helpful to articulate your motivations for making a career move, so it can be enlightening to undertake the exercise of discovering how many times you have already acted as a consultant.

Questions to ask: What were the times I exercised my best judgment and made a recommendation to the team? On what occasions did I take away a stack of background documentation and return later with an assessment and a plan? How often was I the one to do the background research so we could figure out what others had done in situations similar to ours?

TIP

Insight into personality types comes in handy with clients, too. Being able to gauge your clients' personalities is helpful in terms of suggesting how to build a productive relationship. For example, big-picture types and detail-oriented types react differently to information we give them about the progress of a project: understanding where the "hot buttons" are can help avoid unnecessary misunderstanding, and knowing someone's style and process of internalizing new information is extremely useful when it comes to crafting the progression of a document's messages. Watching people interact in the client setting helps us obtain much valuable input to guide us as we interact with them.

Part Two

Getting
Established
and
Getting Down
to Business

Business Planning

Is There a Market—and a Living—for Me?

Anecdotal (and I might add, personal) evidence suggests that it *is* possible to "just do it" and embark upon a successful consulting career with little in the way of formal planning. As a *strategy*, though, such an approach would be at odds with most of the advice out there. There is no downside to planning ahead—and considerable upside.

Every commercial and public sector organization must somehow generate revenue or funding. When it comes to financial viability, being a consultant is the same as being a spa owner: if the target market desires the services and benefits offered and has the means and willingness to pay, there is a business. Thus the success factor for consultants ought to boil down to the fundamental market truth that those who identify and meet a need will be able to secure customers. In reality, it is more complex. There may well be a market with a need for our services, but that market—for various reasons—may not be able to pay for them (or pay at a level where we can make a living).

What Do I Want to Do?

Precision in the definition of your future consulting practice is an immediate requirement. At a conference, private party, or community meeting, answering the question "So what do you do?" needs more than "I'm a consultant." Let's add a specific description of services: "I help my clients deal with . . ."; "My firm specializes in . . ."; "I design . . ."

Mind you, many consultants will share how they imagined themselves offering a particular line of services but gradually added others. Expect that, over time, the specifics of your services could change as client challenges evolve and your own experience and interests evolve too.

What Is the Size of the Potential Market?

Documenting the existence of a market need for the services we intend to offer is a fundamental instrument in planning. We must create a scenario on the basis of statistics, industry studies, trade journals, and input from colleagues. The questions we raise as we build the scenario include the following:

- ■ What types of organizations do I expect to need my services?
- ■ Specifically, am I targeting certain departments within such organizations?
- ■ How many such organizations are there in the geographic or cyberspace area I could reach?
- ■ What is known about typical consulting assignments in the target market (e.g., scope, compensation ranges)?

What Are the Trends in the Business Sector I Want to Focus On?

Where a particular sector—say, large public libraries—is targeted, you may already be familiar with the business conditions that can be expected in it and with the relevant sources of information about it. If you have a broader aim—say, human resources development—it becomes a bit trickier to identify signs that, indeed, there is a sufficient market. Whatever the field, we librarians have an advantage: we know how to do research. So, undaunted, we prepare an overview of the outlook in the intended sector (as illustrated in chapter 2).

How Are Consultants Currently Doing in the Intended Market?

The most important probe targets others who are now doing what you would like to be doing in the future. Library professionals are generally considered strong networkers who readily share their insights with others; it should be straightforward to set up interviews with colleagues. To be sure, some might legitimately be concerned about the prospect of new competitors; it is, however, equally likely that established consultants will welcome having access to new subcontractors or new colleagues to suggest to clients when their workload is too great.

You will want to hear what consultants have to say about questions such as these:

- How much conventional work experience did you have when you started?
- Did you have clients lined up in advance?
- How do you now find clients—or they you?
- Are there types of clients and assignments you prefer, and if so why?
- How do you expect the market to evolve in the future? Is there enough work for more consultants?
- What is your workload like in terms of volume?
- Are there seasonal variations, budget and planning cycles, or other fluctuations to be aware of?
- Are there lessons learned or "if I were to do it over" stories?

Though colleagues are likely to offer insight into many details you didn't know to ask about, there could be a tendency on their part not to dwell on the most challenging or least favorite aspects of their lives as consultants. Similarly, the need to protect client confidentiality may limit a consultant's ability to be explicit.

Can I Reach My Target After-Tax Income, Given What I Know about the Market?

Now comes a potentially scary exercise. You must assess the total gross income you need, and whether such a figure is realistic, given the market insight you have gained. In that calculation, it is vital to allow for the considerable time you cannot bill to clients—the time spent in networking, keeping up-to-date in your field, writing proposals, attending conferences, preparing seminars and presentations, writing articles, and so on. It is not uncommon for consultants to say that as much as 60 percent of their total work time is nonbillable. A typical estimate looks like this:

Total amount needed to cover anticipated personal living expenses: _____

Add estimated ongoing business expenses: _____

Assuming an estimated x percent income tax rate, gross billings
  must reach: _____

Assuming 48 weeks $\times$ 5 days = 240 working days in a year,

  if 60 percent billable, divide gross by 144 working days =
  daily rate of: _____

  if 40 percent billable, divide gross by 96 working days =
  daily rate of: _____

Example: You estimate a need to make $70,000 a year for yourself and in addition cover business expenses of $30,000. To reach an after-tax income that will make these requirements comfortably possible (although business expenses are tax deductible, they are paid up front), you determine a need to bill, say, $150,000 a year. That points to a daily rate of just over $1,000 if your time is 60 percent billable, and more than $1,550 if your time is 40 percent billable. You now need to know how such rates compare with rates currently quoted by other consultants.

Important notes: Even though your intention may be to charge fixed fees for specified deliverables, your calculations should be (roughly) translated into work days per year—to test whether the assumptions about the volume of work are physically possible.

If there are *products* (such as proprietary market research reports, books, or similar objects) you can sell to multiple clients with minimum effort on your part, their revenue potential offsets the above calculations.

Once a potential range of daily rates has been calculated, the next questions are

■ How would you feel quoting any of the rates?
■ Is there a risk any given rate could limit opportunities because it is perceived to be too high by the target clientele?
■ Similarly, could a given rate be so low as to signal a lack of confidence in the quality of your work?

If you determine that your "safe" daily rate will not yield the desired annual gross billing, you may need to do some more digging around to resolve the arithmetic. A financial cushion as you start could provide the opportunity to charge somewhat modestly at first, then raise rates as you gain a track record.

What If Business Is Slow to Build?

Plan for a modest income in the early stages of your consulting career, and be realistic in estimating billings for the first few years.

A part-time job could prove valuable as a fallback in the early stages—but it might also limit the time available for business development. Working as a subcontractor to an established consultant may be a productive compromise, letting you earn income while learning the ropes and building a reputation.

Of course, you need some way to make up any income shortfall in the ramp-up period. Your personal savings (or your spouse's income) may keep you going—but do prepare a budget showing how the expenses of the household can be met while you are still working toward your full income potential.

Any financial planner would recommend some basic record keeping in order to establish whether you have any leeway in reducing expenses. Aside from the nonadjustable expenses (such as a mortgage), what are you spending now on nonessentials? Tallying up the small-sounding amounts in situations where there is a cheaper alternative—for example, grabbing a meal at a coffee shop versus taking a sandwich along—could easily have you exclaiming, "I can't believe $1,000 a month goes to stuff I could do without!" (If all you do as a result of reading this primer is get better at managing your money, you're ahead of the game.)

The Business Plan

Small businesses and consultancies require a great deal of personal drive. Vision is necessary, and your business plan is the tool for making that vision clear. Most inspirational speakers and writers stress in their own ways how important it is to be quite specific about what you want and how you plan to go about getting it.

Small businesses and consulting practices differ from each other in that the latter usually require no inventory, warehouse, shipping, storefront, and the like. Thus certain elements in the many published guidelines do not pertain, but it may still be useful to check some tried and true resources for creating business plans. As an example, the U.S. Small Business Administration offers many pointers (www.sba.gov/smallbusinessplanner/plan/writeabusinessplan/index.html). Another useful source is Entrepreneur .com.

In addition, any quick check of book resources such as Amazon.com or your public library will lead you to published books dealing with the subject.

A Business Plan "Alternative"

If you feel the discipline of writing a business plan is too daunting (just yet), you may consider a "personal business statement" as a platform for thinking about your business while you conduct more research. Such a statement is akin to the proverbial elevator speech in that it is brief, but it adds detail about *how* you are going to help your clients. For example:

- Building on my experience in the . . . , I focus on projects in the area of . . .
- I help clients who deal with challenges such as . . .
- My typical approach involves . . .
- My typical deliverable is a . . .

When you have finished reading this primer, you may want to return to the matter of crafting a plan.

Getting Ready
The Building Blocks

Establishing and operating a consultancy involve several formalities prescribed by the jurisdiction in which you live. It is useful to remember that, although you may be a skilled consultant in your area of expertise, other professionals would be better at filing tax forms or creating professional-looking promotional materials. As you build your new business, it pays to invest in the best guidance and specialized services you can find.

USEFUL BOOKMARKS

These sites are particularly rich in resources for the self-employed:

- www.inc.com (check out the articles grouped by topic)
- www.powerhomebiz.com
- www.entrepreneur.com

The Legal Status

You need to register your business in the state, province, or country where you live, and you must ensure that your tax affairs are in perfect order from the beginning. An accountant and an attorney can advise you whether to incorporate or to operate as a sole proprietorship. The filing requirements and tax implications of each are worth examining in depth.

One business option is for two or more individuals to register a partnership. Similar in nature to a sole proprietorship, a partnership has obvious special implications related to division of roles, labor, and income.

Entrepreneur.com's site has a section titled "How to Legally Establish Your Homebased Business." It begins with how to choose the business structure. Although sole proprietorships and partnerships are the most common, you have a choice of entities, each with its advantages and disadvantages. Corporations and limited liability companies, for example, present documentation requirements you may not find appealing.

The Business Name

Constructing a business name from your surname along with "and Associates"—even if there are none—may be a good choice if you haven't already coined a catchy name that conveys what your business does. Consulting rarely lends itself to clever company names the way some other operations do.

In addition, your domain name is critical intellectual property and a valuable asset. Ideally, your domain name is unambiguously recognizable (as I hope www.destricker.com is). You may want to consult a reference such as Stephen Elias and Patricia Gima's *Domain Names: How to Choose and Protect a Great Name for Your Website* (Berkeley, Calif.: Nolo, 2001).

Logo: A Visual Brand Is Powerful

The adage that "perception is reality" applies in numerous contexts including that of your visual brand. You will want an elegant, pleasing, and eye-catching graphic presence for your website, letterhead, report covers, and business cards. You need a suite of electronic templates so you can create proposals, invoices, memos, and reports easily. Engage a good graphic artist who can devise a classy design; don't waste time struggling to piece together a style on your own. You deserve to be represented in the marketplace in a professional manner.

The Business Card

Entrepreneur.com's "Networking" columnist, Ivan Misner, is sure that the lowly business card is one of the best investments you can make: "The business card is the most powerful single business tool—dollar for dollar—you can invest in. It's compact, energy-efficient, low-cost, low-tech, and keeps working for you hours, weeks and even years after it leaves your hands!"

John Williams, Entrepreneur.com's "Image and Branding" columnist, advises a quality card. "Cheaper isn't always better when it comes to first impressions." Pointing to examples of cards that are difficult to read and otherwise fail to communicate clearly, Williams advises keeping the design simple and professional. I would echo the sentiment that the investment in a professionally designed card is well worth it.

TIP

Your visual brand is not the place to cut costs. Cheap-looking business cards and "homegrown" websites send the wrong message. You want to signal that you offer high-quality work through the quality of the appearance you present in the public space. You want to make sure your visual brand readily identifies all your document deliverables as being yours.

In practice, I have found that the most significant value of a business card lies in its ability to help the client find my website. Our cards should state what we do, then provide a prominent URL.

So much for the "fun" part. There is more.

Taxes: Revenue

Tax advisors are quick to point out that a consulting business needs multiple clients. It may be reassuring to have steady business from a single client, but the tax authorities may deem you to be an employee if you have only one or two clients. Do find out what the guidelines are in your jurisdiction.

Naturally, whether your clients provide formal tax slips or not, you must report every item of revenue, including reimbursements received from clients for expenses.

Taxes: Deductible Expenses

As for expense deductions, it is similarly wise to be aware of the guidelines. The key benefits of engaging an accountant to prepare your tax filing are that you do deduct all legitimate expenses while avoiding deductions that could prove problematic.

Lists of typical tax deduction expenses are readily available on the Internet. Note that, in some jurisdictions, certain business expenses are deductible only in part. Here is a generic overview of major expense categories:

Legal/Financial
- Legal fees associated with the business setup or business licenses
- Insurance (e.g., of the home office contents)
- Bank charges and credit card fees
- Accounting fees, including the cost of having your tax return prepared

Business Operations: Home Office
- Special rules apply for the allowable proportion of overall residence expenses (utilities, cleaning, repairs, renovation/ construction); it may be a square footage percentage

- Office tools/supplies: computer(s), software, ink, paper, DVDs, etc.
- Internet access in-office and on the road
- Phones and PDAs

Business Operations: Travel to Client Sites

- Airfare, accommodation, personal meals
- Car expenses: if your personal car is not exclusively used for business, keep a log of "business miles" and deduct an amount per mile, taking gas and wear and tear into account (let the accountant guide you)

Business Operations: Subcontractors

- Any fees paid to others in the effort of serving your clients

Marketing and Client Entertainment

- Website and search engine optimization
- Entertainment and client meals
- Trade shows and conferences

Education and Current Awareness

- Courses or seminars relevant to your business
- Subscriptions and memberships

It goes without saying that your expense evidence must be impeccable. Every receipt should be labeled relative to the categories above; for example, a restaurant lunch receipt might be marked "B. Mercer—marketing—Yorkton proposal" or "B. Mercer—project work—Yorkton." Whatever your approach to managing paper receipts, do it in a way that lets you put your hands on precisely the category and date of any expense, not only this year for tax purposes but years after the fact in case of an audit.

Ask your accountant what categories and subcategories he or she wants you to use in totaling your deductible expenses, and supply your neat and tidy materials well in time for the tax filing deadline.

The bottom line is that the accountant is a must-have—you want to protect your peace of mind.

Tracking Client Accounts and Activities

Simple spreadsheets and logs may serve us perfectly if we work for a small number of clients in larger projects and issue few invoices each year. It could be worth a look at the Entrepreneur.com site, however, to check whether any of the items in the resource called FormNET (www.entrepreneur .com/formnet/) might be helpful. You may only need a few forms, but why create them from scratch if you do not need to?

Banking

A good relationship with a banker is a major advantage. Whatever it takes, you should build a secure trust with your banking institution. Who knows when you may need assistance cashing a foreign check or increasing your line of credit?

Business account. As soon as you have registered your business, set up a separate business bank account in the business name. Be sure that the bank allows for slight variations in the wording of your business name. For example, if the official business name is *A. B. Cee and Associates,* you want the bank to accept checks made out to "AB Cee" or "Cee Associates" or any other unambiguous variation.

Credit card. It is a given that your business must have its own credit card for business-related expenses and purchases. Credit card statements are useful in documenting expenses, although you may have to annotate them to clarify vague entries. As well, paying certain recurring bills (telephones, Internet access, professional subscriptions, etc.) through automatic deduction from the credit card account saves time. Some banks offer special small-business credit cards, sometimes in association with a line of credit.

Line of credit. Absent personal wealth, you will want a business line of credit to manage the timing of client payments and expenses. Over time, you may build up sufficient savings not to need the credit line—but why not have one?

Liability Insurance

Do you need liability insurance? The answer is, "It depends." If your services do not involve a likelihood of damaging property or causing personal injury, you probably do not need insurance. You could, however, consider using contract language to specify limitations in liability in order to minimize the risk of legal complications. Some consultants state in their proposals that their liability is limited to the amount of the project compensation or to some other amount. Professional liability coverage is expensive. If there is no evidence to the contrary, you are probably safe without it.

Some RFPs include a requirement that the bidder have liability insurance in the millions of dollars. That is appropriate if buildings are being constructed, but it is less relevant for the type of work many library consultants do. In some cases, you may get a verbal assurance that the clause is optional. It is worth being certain about what is required and checking with your lawyer about the options.

Health Insurance

Unless you are covered under a spouse's health plan, you will want to purchase health insurance. Your professional association may offer a group plan; otherwise, you are on your own.

Be sure to understand the provisions of your privately purchased group health insurance. For example, your dental plan may cover a visit to the dentist only every nine months, when you had been accustomed to visits every six months (in which case you must cover the difference personally). Research the coverage offerings carefully, and remember—you are worth a good health insurance plan, expensive as it may be.

Office Support

As a sole consultant, you will need a support network of people to lean on. Let's round out the list of building blocks with a brief overview of basic supports:

Service contract with a computer expert. Unless you have a computer technology background, do not assume that you are the one to find the best computer for your purposes, install software, and perform regular maintenance. Keeping a computer running trouble free is not for amateurs. The cost of having a computer expert visit your office every few months (to update the virus checker, upgrade software, etc.) is a wise investment, and you will be glad you have someone to call on when the computer crashes. You stand to lose weeks of precious time if you are without access to someone qualified to restore your operations. (In fact, see if your service supplier will keep duplicate backup CDs or DVDs for you.)

Communications gadgets. With so many offerings on the market, seek advice on and shop carefully for the most suitable combination of landline and cell phone plans and on-the-road access to e-mail and the Internet.

Operational support. If you need it, get help with clerical tasks such as expense logging, bookkeeping, filing, certain kinds of routine research, and the like.

Your personal network. One of the benefits of working in an office is the constant interaction with others. Working independently can cut us off from its stream of news and small talk, so we need to take steps to make sure we stay connected with our peers and stay aware of relevant industry developments. To that end, it is wise to subscribe to the relevant newsletters and trade journals. Be sure to sign up for relevant discussion groups. Trade shows, association meetings, and seminars are other useful means of staying in touch and keeping your professional network active. The associated expenses are tax deductible, so there is no reason to deprive yourself.

Finally: Keep Checking the Web

The following short list of URLs is but a small sampling to illustrate the range of resources for small and home businesses; even though they are not specific to consulting, they are good sources of practical information.

GOVERNMENT ORGANIZATIONS AND ASSOCIATIONS

American Library Association (www.ala.org)

Association of College and Research Libraries (www.acrl.org)

Association of Independent Information Providers (www.aiip.org)

Canadian Library Association (www.cla.ca)

National Association for the Self-Employed (www.nase.org)

National Federation of Independent Business (www.nfibonline.com)

Special Libraries Association (www.sla.org)

Strategis (http://strategis.ic.gc.ca)

U.S. Small Business Administration (www.sba.gov)

SMALL BUSINESS RESOURCES

About.com Small Business (http://sbinformation.about.com)

BizMove (www.bizmove.com)

CanadaOne Small Business (www.canadaone.com)

Home Business Magazine (www.homebusinessmag.com)

Microsoft Canada Small Business Corner (www.microsoft.com/canada/smallbiz/)

Microsoft Small Business Center (www.microsoft.com/smallbiz/)

Small Business Advancement National Center (www.sbaer.uca.edu)

SOHO America (www.soho.org)

StartupNation (www.startupnation.com)

MARKETING

Duct Tape Marketing (www.ducttapemarketing.com)

Guerrilla Marketing Online (www.gmarketing.com)

Marketing Library Services (www.infotoday.com/mls/)

YOUR WEB PRESENCE

Canadian Web Hosting Directory (http://ca.webhostdir.com)

Domain Fellow (www.domainfellow.com)

Domain Name Wizard (http://dnwiz.com)

Find Web Hosts (http://thewhir.com/find/web-hosts/)

RegistrarStats (www.registrarstats.com)

RegSelect (www.regselect.com)

SitePoint (www.sitepoint.com)

7

Getting Out There

Marketing
a Personal Brand

Planning far ahead and building relationships with one's first clients while still having the security of employment are probably not the norm. Still, whether the planning phase is long or short (or nonexistent), certain strategies can be adopted by anyone wanting an improved professional profile.

In my own case, I "accidentally" prepared for a consulting career throughout my years of employment in the information industry. First, I had customer-facing positions, so getting known by many people came naturally; conducting hundreds of workshops though many years adds up to a fair amount of visibility. Second, I was active in the relevant professional association, holding various offices. Third, I wrote numerous articles and became a familiar figure on the podium at conferences. None of this was done with a deliberate plan in mind to one day become a consultant, but in retrospect it laid the foundation for the credibility I enjoyed from the very first day I undertook a client project. I am, then, in a position to state that getting out there and creating a professional profile is essential for anyone considering a consulting career.

Build a Reputation

Possibly the strongest marketing tool we can create for ourselves is name recognition and a reputation for quality. When colleagues mention us to a potential client, the reaction should be "Oh yes, I have heard wonderful things about her!" A strong "brand" among peers who will be providing referrals and among those who could become clients is an essential foundation for credibility as a consultant. Do not hesitate—if you haven't already engaged in them, these tried and true techniques are waiting for you to get started:

Be a volunteer: How may I serve? Leaders in professional associations—especially at the local chapter levels—often lament the increasing difficulty of recruiting volunteers to serve on committees and boards. One phone call or e-mail should get you launched on your association career—and do consider that clients will look favorably upon a track record as "Chair of this" and "Member of the board of that."

Write: How may I share? Many editors of association-related bulletins comment that they are constantly begging for contributions; similarly, editors of trade and professional journals are always on the lookout for new and fresh material to keep subscribers feeling they are getting value for the subscription fee. Why not answer the call? If no specific topic is burning a hole in your keyboard, ask the editors what they feel might be of interest to the readership. Consider some common types of articles in the professional literature:

> *Project descriptions:* Help others by telling the story of your objectives, how you did it, what you achieved, and what you learned (without revealing confidential information, of course).
>
> *New tools and resources:* Save readers time through mini-tutorials on the ins and outs of new market offerings or web tools relevant for them.
>
> *Issues and challenges:* Cut through the confusion and ambiguity and offer guidance applicable to commonly encountered situations across the range of legal, ethical, technical, and client relations challenges common in the library and knowledge management world.

Organizational strategy: Shed light on the dynamics and "politics" that may be causing members of the profession to lose sleep. Share your successes in communication, team building, project management—all those skills most of us did not have the opportunity to learn in an academic setting.

Speak: How may I inspire? Why not build a dynamite presentation from the article you just finished writing? Conference organizers are responsible for delivering engaging programs to their audiences and welcome opportunities for offering fresh contributions. If you feel intimidated, start by presenting at local association events. At all times stay in touch with those who are serving on program committees.

In fairness, it should be stated that speaking at conferences cannot be assumed to generate business. The attendees in the session may be wowed by your presentation but may not be in a position to engage consultants (although they could potentially mention you to those in that position). It is best to regard podium presence as an effort toward establishing a professional reputation in general.

What about a Soon-to-Be Former Employer?

It is well known that we should avoid competing against an immediate former employer, but if you will be offering noncompeting services no complications should arise. If you do intend to offer services similar in nature to those of your ex-employer, a wise approach is to be open about your plans so that an appropriate legal arrangement can be made.

It is always a good idea to ask colleagues whether they are interested in staying in touch. They could be valuable members of your professional network.

Marketing? What Marketing?

For many consultants, the brand-, visibility-, and reputation-related efforts described above succeed in attracting business. The general sense is that many traditional marketing techniques are nonstarters: "I have never secured an engagement through any means other than personal referral" is a common statement, and the question "How do you market your services?" sometimes gets a "What marketing?" exclamation.

The academic discipline of professional services marketing has produced a treasure trove of literature. Most of us, however, are not operating quite in the sphere of the global firms that are a common focus of that literature. Thus, consultants treat marketing as a craft tailored uniquely to their clients and services. Again, you will do well to seek the advice of someone who is well established.

Delighted Clients Are Our Best Marketers

Happy clients may not think to offer to market our services. After all, their focus is the project they hired us for. That does not stop us from asking, "Would you mind putting your name to an endorsement?" Should the client be willing but signal that time is an issue, we can offer to craft a suggestion based on the success of the assignment; chances are the client will be glad to sign. Some clients may want to remain anonymous—in which case we use generic designations such as "CEO, large metropolitan public library."

Word of Mouth Reigns Supreme

The phone rings, or there's an e-mail: "John Barek suggested you might be able to assist in a project we are considering—or perhaps you can recommend someone." You bet. We proceed immediately to learn about the project and to ascertain whether this is one we would like to bid on.

Because word of mouth is so important, consultants value their relationships with other consultants for the referral function. The old adage "one good turn deserves another" is definitely true. Be sure to feed information back to your referrers so they know in the future what kind of projects they can confidently bring to your attention.

Should You Advertise? What about Directory Listings?

Given the effectiveness and prevalence of personal referral, some consultants question the need for and the results of traditional advertising, commenting that an article in a trade journal is a better instrument for drawing attention to their services. "An advertisement makes a claim—an article substantiates it."

Being listed in the appropriate directories, on the other hand, is always advisable regardless of any impression that no one picks a consultant out of a directory. It can't possibly do any harm.

The Website

It is important to be able to direct potential clients to a website that clearly describes the nature of our services. Such a description offers prospective clients a chance to get oriented about the type of projects we specialize in and to get a sense of the clientele we serve. New clients will expect to find a professionally designed and easily navigated site containing these elements at a minimum:

- Narrative description of the types of services we offer
- Indication of the types of challenges we help clients address
- Representative selection of previous assignments and key accomplishments
- List of clients (separate from the assignment list)—with names for those who agree to be listed and generic descriptions for those who prefer not to be named
- Links to articles and presentations
- Information about our educational background and professional experience

Value-added content such as a newsletter or blog can be a tool for keeping a following of interested individuals returning to the site—and, we hope, for being the subject of collegial commentary ("I thought this was interesting; here's the link"). Some consultants use their websites to sell, for example, copies of books or reports.

The work of creating and maintaining a professional services website is not trivial. Unless your services include the design of websites—in which case you will naturally want to demonstrate that very skill—it makes sense to engage professionals who can achieve a reflection of the quality of the work you do.

The contrary view. Some consultants say, "I made it this far without a website, and I'm not inclined to do all that work so long as business comes to me." It is certainly possible to be successful without a web presence—but for someone setting out as a new consultant (as opposed to having decades of reputation to build on), a good website is the way to go. For new consultants the question is, Would my potential clients find me credible without a high-quality website?

Proposals and Contracts

Documenting the Business Relationship

onsultants often comment that one steep learning curve for them was creating such instruments as proposals and contract documents. Indeed, there is an art to expressing precisely what you offer to do for and deliver to a client, and to crafting the final agreement between two parties in a business relationship.

Proposals

Is a written proposal always needed? Even though you and your client are in complete verbal agreement as to the proposed project, a proposal document may be required for several reasons, one of which could be that your direct client needs to "shop it upstairs" for approval at a higher level. Therefore, it pays to hone your skills in developing clear, easy to understand, and effective proposals. By "effective," I mean that they sell the ultimate client on the benefits of proceeding.

Are proposals always free? Some proposals are quite complex and time consuming, and one approach could be to offer the client a free "service offer memorandum" including a quote for preparing a detailed proposal. The fee for the proposal preparation could then, as a gesture of goodwill, be deducted in part from the project fee if the project proceeds.

A proposal should include the following sections:

Background: Understanding of the project. In an introductory section, outline the circumstances and drivers leading to the need for assistance in order to illustrate that you understand the motivation for the project. In this section, emphasize (1) the risks, challenges, or opportunities the client is experiencing, and (2) the fact that your firm can deliver the desired results. The Background section is meant to reassure the reader up front that "I understand your situation—I'm your solution" or "I understand you want to capitalize on an opportunity—I can help make it happen." It is important to use language that resonates with the reader's concerns; in other words, *the Background section speaks to meeting a specific need already recognized.* The degree to which you suggest possibilities for expanding the scope of the originally described project depends on several factors, such as how well you know the client. Some potential clients may react negatively to a premature "upsell" in this portion of the proposal document.

Consultant qualifications and relevant previous projects. To a brief but powerful description of your credentials and experience, add a short list of projects sufficiently similar to the one at hand that it's clear the client is getting, if not an "old hand," then at least someone familiar with the territory. Depending on your previous clients' preferences, the list may be specific or generic ("ABC Law Firm Library" or "medium-sized law firm library").

References. With explicit permission from previous clients (for the proposal at hand or ideally for any future proposal), list the name, title and affiliation, and e-mail and phone number of those in a position to comment on your work. (The conclusion of a successful project is a good time to ask, "May I from now on use your name as a reference whenever I need to?" The likely answer is yes, especially if you assure that you will describe the project in such a way as to respect competitive intelligence and confidentiality concerns.)

Proposed approach. Describe in high-level terms how you propose to go about the project (the work steps come later). You may, for instance, indicate that "a proven methodology is suggested" and go on to outline its key elements. (Even though the suggested approach is obvious to you, it may not be so to the client or the client's senior management.) This section is intended to reassure the reader that you have solved similar challenges and that you have a firm plan in mind. If relevant, this is the place to mention that budgetary constraints point to a preliminary rather than an exhaustive scope—so that it is clear your proposed approach is not necessarily the ideal one but rather reflects reality.

Client support. It is vital to be up front about what your proposed approach requires from the client. Some needs may be quite basic, amounting to nothing more than the use of a desk and a meeting room and access to relevant documentation. Should you require more significant involvement as well, the proposal specifies, for example, "access to relevant IT personnel who will assume responsibility for . . ." or "assistance in terms of arranging the logistics of staff interviews." The key is to spell out in detail what you expect the client to provide.

Work steps, estimated work effort, and time line. Clients appreciate seeing a work plan for the activities you will undertake and a time line of work days and elapsed time. Such a plan clarifies the scope of effort and sets the stage for the upcoming fee quotation. In addition, it lets you show the client that you are taking into consideration non-project-related realities such as holidays and approval process delays (if an approval of a mid-project document or design takes longer than anticipated, the remaining project time line is affected accordingly). Be sure to use dates with caution: "Ten weeks after initiation" is a better formulation than "October 31" because you have no control over the initiation date. It is important to preface any time line overview with commentary to the effect that unforeseen events, client assessment of interim deliverables, new discoveries deemed worthy of further attention, and similar factors may affect the time line, and that the proposed durations are intended as an illustration only. Naturally, you could add that certain optional client contributions may speed up the time line (e.g., if the client supplies personnel to execute a survey and tabulate the results, you save time).

Deliverables. This section could be the trickiest part of a proposal. *What,* exactly, will the client have in hand when the project is finished? A blueprint? A recommendation for developing a new product or service?

A staff training plan? A marketing campaign plan? A scheme for indexing internal documents into the corporate repository? What level of *granularity* will your deliverable have? For example, are you sketching an overall strategic direction for others to use as guidance in creating work plans, or are you offering to develop the work plans? Similarly, it is important not only to describe the *nature* of the deliverable but also to indicate its *size;* "overview" could mean a two-page memo to you but in the client's mind imply a ten-pager. It is better to say in the proposal "an outline in the eight-page range" and then deliver ten or twelve pages than to disappoint a client who thought an outline was a twenty-page affair.

Be careful not to bind yourself to deliverables that turn out, in the progression of the project, to be inappropriate. For example, suppose the client requested, and you quoted on, an examination and recommendation for the harmonization of multiple databases. As you begin working, you discover that half of the databases are being deemed defunct by the IT staff and will be archived. Events and realities beyond your control may render you unable to perform the full extent of an activity you had in the proposal committed to do, prior to you or the client knowing all the relevant realities. On the other hand, the proposal could hold open a door for clients to ask for services and deliverables different from the ones originally requested. ("Adjustments can be negotiated should opportunities emerge that are not known at the outset.")

"Best effort." You may want to include a statement that your services do not guarantee any specific outcomes beyond the submission of your specified deliverables. In other words, you can commit to producing recommendations, but you have no control over what happens after you deliver them. Similarly, your proposal should not imply that you guarantee to fix a particular problem. Realistically, you can offer to devise a recommended strategy and describe a series of action steps; you cannot promise any specific effect. Check with other consultants in your field to find out if there are commonly used cautionary clauses to consider including in your proposals.

Proposed fees. Some consultants have no difficulty here, quoting exactly what they want and knowing there are plenty of clients willing to pay such fees. Other consultants are concerned about the salability of the proposal. The key here is that you must know what you are worth and whether you are willing to compromise.

Fees: What Am I Charging For? How Much?

Just as your visual brand sends signals about your sophistication as a business professional, so your fees tell a story about your value. Undercharging raises doubts about the quality of work delivered, but you may have legitimate concerns about scaring potential clients off if the quoted fees are high in their view. Another consideration is that you do not wish to compromise your peers; lowballing does a great disservice to your colleagues, and ultimately to all consultants.

A note on the extent of budget negotiations. Your negotiation can be a brief exchange or a drawn-out process involving multiple proposal revisions, depending on the sector, the budget, and the corporate culture. If you do hear, "I can't tell you what the budget is—you tell me what it will cost," be prepared for significant time to pass before a budget figure emerges.

Units. Depending on the nature of your consulting, you may choose to quote your fee as an hourly or a daily rate. Generally consultants quote in daily rates because few consulting assignments are so short as to involve less than several days. Ongoing as-needed brief advice or other assistance such as drafting memos could be tallied on an hourly rate.

Packages. You may want to offer clients the opportunity to prepurchase packages of days at a discount. As an example, if the "rack rate" is x per day, then you might offer five days at 90 percent of $5x$, ten days at 85 percent of $10x$, and so on.

Fixed fees. Many clients appreciate a fixed quote for budgeting reasons. It is helpful to offer several options for consideration (the bronze-silver-gold approach), as in "high-level strategic pointers" versus a "detailed action plan." A single take-it-or-leave-it figure may close the door to an assignment; it is always possible to tailor a service offer to a stated budget. When the client, for whatever reason, is unable to indicate a budget, it is particularly important to offer some options.

Options of scale. You might offer clients the opportunity to consider less costly options for some elements in the proposal.

COST OPTIONS EXAMPLE

In a proposal for conducting an information audit, the fee is influenced in part by how many interactions there are with informants (stakeholders, staff, and all other relevant individuals giving input). You could offer a potential client a choice in this element of the quote, as shown here:

Investigation scope of twenty interviews or focus groups:
$x

Investigation scope of thirty-five interviews or focus groups:
$x + 30 percent

In other words, show the client that there is "more input for the money" in the larger scope—a win-win because the client gets a larger sample into the study and you may not be concerned about working a few more days to achieve a larger compensation. (Given that not 100 percent of days are billable, in reality the choice could be between earning a larger overall fee or doing nothing billable on the "extra" days.) I hasten to add that the scope of the interpretation and recommendations phases of an information audit will probably be unaffected by the input option the client chooses.

Options matrix for service. In my practice, I have seen that potential clients are pleased with a sliding-scale illustration of potential project element scopes and outcomes. For example, in certain project elements, there can be choices of scope for work done by the consulting team and work done by the client's staff.

OPTIONS MATRIX EXAMPLE 1: SCOPE OF EFFORT

In a proposal for conducting a probe of potential public library users' interests and preferences, the following options could be presented:

Scenario 1. FULL SERVICE, for $x: The consulting team will design, test, conduct, and categorize the input from twenty focus groups.

Scenario 2. SERVICE WITH CLIENT SUPPORT, for 50 percent of $x: The consulting team will design, test, and conduct five focus groups, with client staff in attendance to learn the process. Client staff will then conduct fifteen sessions and provide raw notes from each session.

Scenario 3. COACHING LEVEL, for 30 percent of $x: The consulting team will design, test, and conduct three focus groups, with client staff in attendance to learn the process. Consultants will provide detailed guidance for the categorization of the session input. Client staff will conduct seventeen sessions and provide categorized notes from each, grouped according to demographic clusters.

Although it may be attractive for the client to select the less expensive options resulting from engaging staff, it should be kept in mind that staff members may bring "baggage" to the project and thus lack objectivity. In scenario 2, for example, the notes coming back to the consultants may be unconsciously screened and weighted in such a way that the consultants are on a weaker footing when it comes to preparing recommendations. (The purpose of consultants, in the first place, is to ensure candor and neutrality; greater staff involvement could introduce some compromise here.) Or, in scenario 3, the client loses the advantage that consultants often see implications and opportunities staff members may not see because they are too close to the situation.

Options for deliverables. Just as we may offer options in terms of the scope of the work to be performed, we may also offer several possibilities in terms of the nature, extent, and detail of the deliverable.

OPTIONS MATRIX EXAMPLE 2: DELIVERABLES

Using the above scenarios, we could now quote as follows in terms of deliverables:

Deliverable Option 1. High-level summary of priorities expressed and strategic pointers to types of services thereby indicated as being essential versus nice to have. (In this case, the client must figure out what to do next.)

Deliverable Option 2. Detailed summary of priorities expressed and specific pointers to types of services the library should consider developing or enhancing, including examples from similar communities. (In this case, the client has much more to go on in terms of planning.)

Deliverable Option 3. (A) Detailed summary of priorities expressed and specific pointers to types of services the library should consider developing or enhancing, including examples from similar communities. (B) Strategic plan and business plan for implementation. (In this case, the client can proceed to budget approval and implementation.)

What about out-of-pocket expenses? If you provide research information to the client, your direct costs for searches are significant expenses to be covered by the client. But in many consulting assignments, expenses are sufficiently trivial that billing for them would seem odd. In such cases, a safe option is to have the overall fee cover routine minor outlays (local travel, the occasional meal).

Travel. The client cannot be held responsible for your choice of residence—yet you cannot be expected to foot the cost of extensive travel. If you and your client are far apart geographically, it must be clear who pays what expenses. Opportunities for inexpensive travel should be seen in light of the extra stress and fatigue. "Spending an extra seven hours in the airport for the cheaper fare was a viable option when I was younger!"

An allowance for travel expenses can work well for clients. No one needs to get involved in the details of flights and hotels, and we consultants may benefit from the opportunity to add personal days to a professional visit (paying the extra costs ourselves).

If you work with a nonlocal client on a regular basis, make sure your business arrangement accommodates the distance. For example, driving three hours each way multiple times should be compensated somehow.

Subcontractors. Naturally, your overall quote reflects the fees you pay to subcontractors. But do not underestimate the effort and cost of turning subcontractors' work into your own deliverable. Time-consuming editing is a realistic expectation. In some cases, you may have an agreement with subcontractors that you share the work and the fees (according to some formula) without regard to hour-by-hour activity. When you work with a new subcontractor for the first time, it is especially important that you protect yourself: you don't want to pay for what you expected to be deliverables close to your own standard only to sit up nights fixing up an unusable document or struggling with formatting challenges.

Contingency plans if requested. Some clients may want security that, if you fall ill, the project will carry on. If you are featuring a team in the proposal, it makes sense to state that team members can perform the project work even if you should become unavailable for medical or other emergency reasons (note: going off on other projects does not count). It shows strength when you can demonstrate how your team will deliver, no matter what. If you are a solo, it is wise to state that a trusted colleague can step in for you in case of an emergency.

The RFP: What Are the Chances?

Sooner or later, you are likely to need to decide whether to respond to an RFP. In some specialty areas, RFPs are the standard way in which clients reach and select consultants. Consider the following in the context of your business:

Some RFPs are instruments for client orientation in that there may not be any firm commitment to proceeding. In other words, the issuing entity will defer a final decision on the potential project until responses have been received. As a consequence, consultants may be reluctant to put too much effort and detail into their responses.

The RFP may set out a structure for the proposal document that is sufficiently different from that of your customary proposals that significant work is needed to fit the pieces into place. In addition, it may require some ingenuity to insert elements you consider important over and above the sections or chapters the RFP explicitly demands. (One approach I have used is to show in each section title the number of the section in the RFP that is being specifically addressed.)

The RFP may stipulate requirements so specific and detailed that it is difficult to prove they can be met. Moreover, you may feel that a different approach than the one spelled out in the RFP would in fact be preferable—and a bid in response to an RFP may not be a good place to present that view.

Sometimes, possibly because of the complexity of preparing the RFP, it is published so close to the bid due date that bidders have little time to prepare a responding bid.

If you feel you have a good shot at being awarded a project, you may regard it as a good investment of time to prepare a bid. The bottom line: The RFP bidding process is quite complex, often involving bidders' conferences, rounds of written questions and answers, or both. Until you become familiar with the process, seek the advice of someone with experience.

Contracts

In the public sector, standard contracts full of legal jargon are common. In the private sector, a simple purchase order attached to the consultant's proposal is sometimes used as the contract. Some clients issue their own contracts, often with excerpts from your original proposal as a "statement of work"; other clients may ask if you have a standard contract. Regardless of the specific practice being followed, it is to everyone's advantage when the contract is clear about what is being delivered for the specified fee. For example, it is usually wise to spell out the following:

What are the start and end dates for the project? Are such dates fixed or variable according to certain conditions? What allowance is there for changing dates (e.g., the emergence of circumstances unknown at the outset)?

What will be delivered in the course of the project? Whether the deliverable is a tangible item (e.g., a survey report) or an event (e.g., the planning and execution of a conference), details should be given so that expectations are clear. Always clarify the scope of a deliverable to avoid misunderstanding (e.g., "a three-hour seminar for twenty participants" as opposed to "a workshop").

Is there a schedule or elapsed time plan? What are the provisions and opportunities for adjustments should unforeseen events occur?

What materials and personnel resources will the client offer the consultant?

What are the details of payment? For example, is there an upfront initiation fee? (Note that such upfront fees are uncommon in the public sector, and that they are typical of larger projects.) Are there interim payments associated with interim deliverables?

Are there out-of-pocket expenses to be billed, or is there an overall fixed allowance for such expenses as travel and accommodation?

Are there taxes to be collected, or is the client exempt? (Examples are the Canadian GST—Goods and Services Tax; and the European VAT—Value Added Tax.)

Are there confidentiality provisions?

What recourse is available in case of unforeseen circumstances? Some contracts contain a section outlining the common assumptions underlying the engagement and describing the process to be invoked if there is a complication. It is wise to investigate how similar consultants protect themselves from potential difficulty through contract provisions—without running the risk of calling undue attention to a hypothetical situation that is highly unlikely to develop.

Subcontracting

It is common for consultants to prepare joint proposals or for a consultant to indicate in a proposal that subcontractors are part of the team. Regardless of the type of contract you have with your colleagues—a handshake or a legal document—it must be made clear to clients what role the subcontractors play. If it is not known at the outset whether subcontractors will be needed, the project contract language can allow for the possibility of engaging them, on client approval.

In some cases, you may outsource some pieces of work—for example, you could hire someone to put together a bibliography you don't have time to work on yourself. It is always a good idea to indicate such arrangements in a proposal.

Of course, any consultant is responsible for the quality of subcontractors' work, and we want to protect the trust clients have in us by making sure any deliverable is up to our own standard.

9

So Tell Me

What's It Really Like?

Employment is associated with job descriptions, lists of duties, and in some cases procedure manuals. If formal procedures aren't documented, there is generally a set of guidelines according to which the work of the position gets carried out—so that the incumbent has a sense of there being a right way to go about the tasks. All of that goes out the window when we hang out our consulting shingles; we are left with nothing but our knowledge, experience, common sense, and creativity. Curious colleagues are likely to wonder "how we do it," and many a consultant has replied to the question by saying something to the effect of, "I couldn't tell you. I just follow my instincts and do what I think is best for the client."

But wait, our colleagues say, there must be some overall features and characteristics of consulting assignments. In an effort to provide a glimpse of the "consulting life," I offer an overview of a sequence of events that would be typical of many assignments.

I stress that some of the commentary in this chapter is most relevant for projects in which the consultant is asked to provide solutions to complex operational or creative challenges, as opposed to projects whose details are more predictable. I do not wish to project a message that consulting is fraught with stress or controversy; however, the reality in many cases is that, in the words of several of my colleagues, "We are organizational psychologists disguised as library consultants."

Six Stages to the Contract

The outline below illustrates a progression of events common to many consulting assignments. But, as the advertisements say, "Your mileage may vary."

STAGE 1
IS THIS THE KIND OF WORK YOU DO?

Consultants quickly learn to love calls or e-mail from complete strangers—the caller or writer may be inquiring whether we could be a good fit. "We're looking for someone who can help prepare a marketing and communications plan for the library and Jason Cox mentioned your name." There are two "correct" responses to such an opening: "Yes—now or in a little while," or "I'm not certain I can help you, but I will put you in touch with someone who can."

Even if you sense the project is not in your area of specialty, don't lose an opportunity to impress a potential client. Obtain enough background information to determine who in your professional network might be relevant. You are the judge of how much time you invest in finding the best consultant for the client—keeping in mind the benefit of being able to extend a favor to a colleague that may one day get repaid.

In the interest of encouraging referrals, the practice of offering the referrer a finder's fee can be recommended. Close colleagues who refer each other frequently may elect to omit courtesy rewards, feeling no need for such accounting.

STAGE 2
EXPLORING THE POTENTIAL ASSIGNMENT:
STATED OBJECTIVES VS. TRUE NEEDS

Some prospective clients clearly articulate what they are looking for; others are much more tentative. It is important to gain, as early as possible, a sense not only of the type of work the assignment would entail but also of how firmly the client appears to be attached to a particular approach. These questions are in the back of our minds as we enter into discussions:

> Is the client asking for a concrete, preconceived deliverable—or for advice and guidance in the context of a particular challenge?

Does the client seem open to constructive input even before there is a business relationship?

If you feel the client is asking for the wrong thing, you can be bold and say, "In my judgment, based on what you have told me, I believe you need something different from what you are requesting. I would not feel comfortable quoting a fee for a service I doubt will meet your true needs."

Here's an illustration. The potential client who inquired about a marketing and communications plan for the library might in fact be much better off having a strategic plan for services aligned with the preferences and practices of key target market groups—before any marketing takes place. In other words, you may conclude from an initial discussion that the client has overlooked the fact that marketing is unlikely to succeed if the services being promoted do not match market needs. What do you do? Several scenarios could play out; here are two:

> *Scenario 1:* Confirm that you have created many such plans in the past and would be perfectly able to come up with another. Then inquire as to what market research has been performed in the area of target market needs: "Just so we are sure we are marketing and communicating about services the target groups actually need and want, may I ask about the input you possess to suggest that your library is in fact offering services aligned with constituent needs?" If the reply indicates a weakness in the area of market research, you can then pursue the value-added approach: "I believe I can assist you in a way that will ensure your expenditure for a marketing plan is not wasted." If the client is receptive, your proposal will then include equal emphasis on market research, strategic planning for services based on same, and (finally) marketing efforts.

> *Scenario 2 (much less satisfactory):* Conclude that the client is determined in his or her request and offer to prepare a proposal—in which you will include a stage titled "market need verification" as well as a disclaimer that, without a foundation of insight into market requirements, the success of any marketing campaign is unpredictable.

Again, it is up to the consultant to decide how much effort to put into early discussions. You can always consider referring to a colleague and offering your colleague a full debrief.

Should we determine that we want to proceed in the potential business relationship, we could offer to prepare a preliminary outline-of-service document—unless we are ready to produce a formal proposal document (stage 5).

STAGE 3
INITIAL OFFER OF SERVICE

Prior to offering any service, it is important to know the answer to this question: Is the person with whom we are speaking about the potential project also the person who will be paying the bill? In other words, who is the ultimate audience for our preliminary offer and subsequent formal proposal? An executive summary section—focused on overall and longer-term benefits rather than on project process—should be included in any document that might need further approval.

The offer-of-service document is intended to give the client a sense of the possibilities rather than to state specific actions and fees. In fact, it may be wise to avoid discussing fees until the client signals a level of comfort with your proposed approach.

STAGE 4
HOW MUCH?

Generally, experienced private sector clients are well prepared to suggest a budget envelope; public sector clients may be restricted by administrative rules in terms of the size of project they can authorize. In the latter case, it is up to the consultant to decide if the available envelope is adequate and worth the effort of bidding on the assignment. But sometimes it is understandable that the client may have no firm sense of the scope of effort involved in a potential project, and the "budget dance" begins. In fact, we sometimes begin consulting long before we are hired because we guide the client through the possible budget options.

It is appropriate to ask the client where the "pain point" is: for example, "My impression is that we are in the $25,000 ballpark at a minimum. Does that agree with your impression?"

If the client does not supply a budget envelope, we are left to estimate a fee that is not so low as to suggest lack of depth and not so high as to eliminate ourselves from the running. As noted earlier, we can consider giving clients the opportunity to review a table of potential options—for amount *a* you will get *x*; amount *b* gets you *y*; and so on.

When a client objects that the quoted fees are too high, it is vital that we do not cave in and reduce the fees arbitrarily, and that we ask "how much too high?" We may then choose to offer services tailored to a lower budget—or abandon the effort altogether. It is better to walk away from a potential project than to subject oneself to unreasonable terms.

STAGE 5
THE FORMAL OFFER (IF NEEDED)

Unless the project is based on a handshake, a formal proposal—one that will stand the potential scrutiny of one or more management committees in the client organization—is needed (see chapter 8). In preparing your proposal, you may need to address officially the quandary described in stage 2: Is what the client wants really what the client needs? Some consultants feel it is against their professional ethics to provide a quote for requested services they believe are not in the client's best interests. If they then offer a well-considered proposal with sound suggestions for an approach that differs from the originally stated requirement, the client may outright reject it. One compromise approach is to submit a proposal that incorporates an assessment phase to determine the best strategy, with an option for the client to terminate the engagement at the end of that phase.

STAGE 6
THE CLIENT'S RESPONSE—AND OURS TO IT

Naturally, we wait with varying degrees of bated breath for the client to acknowledge receipt of the proposal we have spent so much time and effort to prepare, and then for a swift, positive response. If extensive discussions have taken place prior to the writing of the proposal, there may be a verbal agreement to proceed, and the proposal is merely a formal expression for the sake of documentation.

Although it is disappointing to wait for an immediate reply, reality says that clients may be dealing with many other priorities and may need to discuss the proposal with others. A wide variety of circumstances can get in the way of a prompt and simple "Thank you and here is the signed contract":

- The individual requesting the proposal delegates the project to someone else.
- The individual requesting the proposal is suddenly reassigned to another department.
- The project must be discussed in a steering committee meeting several weeks from the date of the proposal.
- Those reacting to the proposal realize by reading it that there were elements they had not considered, and they begin rethinking the nature of the project.
- There is a change in senior management, and the new person in charge puts all consulting projects on hold, pending a budgetary and policy review.
- A sudden crisis intervenes and all attention is directed at dealing with it.

If the client is silent, how long should we wait before inquiring, "Have you had a chance to review my proposal and when should I expect a response?" (If the proposal was sent by e-mail, could it be that the client's servers were down that day and your message was among those lost?) An existing relationship with the client could point to a shorter time than might otherwise be considered appropriate. We need a balance between appearing not to care and appearing so eager that the client feels uncomfortable.

Clients who have not previously hired consultants may not appreciate the finer points of the response etiquette we expect. Do not be surprised if the potential client needs extensive time for assessing your proposal. When the response does arrive, it may turn out not to be quite what we had in mind. For example, the client might request revisions, additions, and price changes. In some cases, the asked-for changes and extra content add up to a request for a business case justifying the project in the first place. Such a request could in the end have positive results—for example, if the support for the project ends up being stronger as a result of our supplying the business case—but we may feel dismay at the prospect of having to take a step backward before we can move forward.

The level of additional effort you are willing to put into the sales stage depends on several factors, such as the size of the project, the amount of other work you have lined up, any hunches you may have that this could be a challenging project, and the like. The bottom line may be to rely on a gut instinct as to the likelihood that a successful project will in the end result from the preliminary exchanges with the client.

A protracted exchange could lead to a slippage in the originally estimated time lines, and you may in the course of the delay have entered into other assignments. That is why it is important never to use fixed dates in proposals but rather to indicate elapsed time "after contract start."

Getting Down to Business

Although no two assignments are alike, key elements of the execution of an engagement can be characterized. The following overview is a distillation of my own experience and that of colleagues; it is intended to provide some "tips from the veterans":

THE CLIENT RELATIONSHIP IS PARAMOUNT

If the contract negotiations have taken place with the individual responsible for the execution of the project, a good relationship may already exist on the day the project gets under way. However, it could be that the first meeting with the client is also the first opportunity we get to know each other—and the style in which we each prefer to work. Similarly, the engaging client we know well may turn the project over to a project manager we haven't met. In such a case, the reality is that two perfect strangers now find themselves on a mission to bring a project to a successful conclusion. The sooner they develop a solid comfort level with each other, the better.

Building a relationship of trust and mutual support encompasses many elements. At the beginning, it is important to gain a sense of "what keeps the client up at night" and what in his or her eyes is an attractive outcome. Being aware of some underlying motivations and concerns will at the very least help put things in context if our proposed strategy and actions do not meet with the reaction we had expected. We look for clues to help understand the client's own context:

- Is there more to the project than just getting the work done? For example, do other consequences ride on the outcome?
- Does the client have a particular outcome in mind, and if so why?
- What would make the client look good to superiors?

In addition, it is helpful to form an impression early on of the client's personal style. Some clients quickly become friends; others prefer a more formal style of collaboration. As noted in chapter 4, certain personal characteristics and skills are helpful for a consultant; in the early stages of an assignment, skills in building rapport and mutual understanding are especially valuable. The better the client and the consultant understand each other, the greater the chances the project will develop smoothly. In the end, the client's role is to help the consultant help her; a good relationship makes that possible.

I have found that some clients appreciate being reassured throughout that they made the right choice and appreciate evidence of past experience. Similarly, it can be a comfort for clients to know their challenges are not unique. "In similar assignments, I found it took quite a bit of effort to orient staff about the capabilities of a new system; at some point we will probably want to discuss how we can get your investment to pay off sooner rather than later."

Although the proposal stated what you need from the client, it is a good idea to go over that territory in person. Perhaps you need nothing more than a stack of background documents to start, followed by a series of interviews with relevant staff members who can shed light on the details of the project. But you may need much more than that, and in my experience it has sometimes been a bit of a surprise to the client how much work it is to keep a consultant supplied with input as the project develops. In situations where new information surfaces to suggest a change of strategy, it can be especially time consuming for the client.

Among consultants, some specific challenges are well known, and it is wise to be prepared for them:

> The project manager is called away to put out some other fire, and you are left with fewer opportunities to communicate and to determine that "we are still on the right track."

> You find yourself reporting to someone not in a position to be an effective project authority. Such a situation calls for a great deal of finesse.

> In a meeting with the direct client or project manager, but with the boss or a senior management team in attendance, you find yourself in the middle of a divergence of impressions about aspects of the project. Extreme tact and delicacy are needed, and in particular it is important not to take personally anything that is said. Diplomacy and creativity come in handy.

BEING IN TOUCH:
WHEN, HOW, HOW MUCH?

Some clients give the consultant a charge and then go off to expect results in due time. Others want to be closely involved every step of the way. It is important to understand up front how much detail the client wants to hear about, and how often.

If the client delegates logistics to another staff member, you may be dealing with the logistics coordinator every day while the communication to the client is a weekly or biweekly progress statement. Regular status updates are a good vehicle, not only for reassuring clients that the project is on track, but also for signaling when and why it is slipping (e.g., "Three individuals to be interviewed this week were off sick, and I seek assistance in finding alternate interviewees unless it is acceptable that the schedule be delayed.").

Keep an interaction log showing who you met with and when, what was discussed, and what further action might be called for. For example, it is common to hear, "You should talk to Mark," or "Let us show you how that application works"—resulting in an interview and activity schedule that gets progressively more crowded. Such a log is needed if the client (or the client's boss) should ever be curious about "why it took so long" or "why no one suggested that you speak to Susan"; but it is also a useful tool for consultants in that, when it comes time to quote on a future assignment, it retains the facts our personal memory might want to forget about how long things take in reality.

WORKING WITH THE CLIENT—AND WITH EVERYONE ELSE IN THE CLIENT'S ORGANIZATION

If asked to point to the one factor that contributes most strongly to their success, consultants are likely to zero in on the relationship with the client: "I like to think of myself as a team member rather than a service provider." "In order to deliver high value, it is imperative to get a really good picture of the client's mix of challenges and the circumstances at hand." "Clients who enable me to understand in depth where they are coming from do themselves a big favor."

From the very first moment, it is desirable that everyone involved with the project—even those who may be only marginally affected—understand precisely the drivers for and nature of the project. A project that is technical in nature (as would be the case when a project deals with library systems, intranets, enterprise content management, etc.) still entails quite a lot of interaction with employees in the client's organization. If there is the slightest perception that "Uh-oh, she's here to pass judgment on how we do our jobs," the result could be a less-than-frank exchange between staff and consultant. Ideally, the client has already oriented staff—but experience shows this is not always the case. Therefore, it is advisable to seek out an early opportunity for an informal conversation to clarify any questions about why the project is being done and how it is intended to unfold. Such an occasion may not only defuse any anxiety but also enable staff members to give some thought to how they might contribute information to help the project along. Even the most experienced consultant may not be in a position to know what questions to ask so as to uncover what is lurking beneath the surface—but staff members well informed about the project can volunteer insight: "Would it be useful if we were to give you a short demo of that part of the intranet?"

In any interaction with client staff, a cardinal rule applies: confidentiality. Interviewees and focus group participants must be assured their input is not going to be quoted by name and will not be reported in any way that exposes them to risk. (Granted, some observations can only have come from a few given sources, and the client is aware of the situation at hand.) The consultant's job is to present objective findings and make recommendations flowing from them. Objective findings (aside from factual evidence, statistics, etc.) are possible only when all personal input is confidential—so that freely given concerns and motivations can be taken into consideration in the overall analysis.

TAKING ADVANTAGE OF NEW OPPORTUNITIES
AS THE PROJECT UNFOLDS

Some projects are cut and dried, without much opportunity for adjustments along the way. Others present opportunities to make changes in strategic direction and thus in the deliverables.

In the earlier commentary about proposals and contracts, we touched on the need for clarity about the nature and size of the deliverables. It is not always the case that a project unfolds precisely as it was anticipated when the engagement took place. As consultants, we owe our clients two things: to deliver what we promised, and to offer to deliver something other and more valuable than what we promised if that opportunity should appear.

In my own experience and that of colleagues, it is not uncommon that during a project information and insights surface which make it appropriate to say, "Shouldn't we take the opportunity to step back and analyze the possible implication of what has surfaced?" Generally it is unrealistic to expect that projects, once under way, can be modified significantly in terms of the budget. There may, however, be room for adjustment in the nature and scope of deliverables.

For example, a challenge first believed to be associated with a specific technical infrastructure may turn out to have much more to do with organizational culture, practices, and individual behaviors. In such a case, the consultant—in my opinion—is morally obliged to so inform the client in order to raise the opportunity to focus efforts where they will truly count. "Although we can press on with the selection of a search engine, we point out that any search engine may have limited value unless attention is paid to current practices in terms of document management." If the client organization's information and knowledge culture presents challenges, no technical tool will solve the situation.

In another example, it might be discovered in the course of a project to determine the best option for upgrading or switching to another integrated library management system that the work flow associated with acquisitions, payment management, and processing of purchases is awkward and—for various historical reasons—contains bottlenecks and superfluous duplication of transactions. Should the consultants simply point out the discovery and plug away at the original charge? Or will the client be receptive to a modification of the project emphasis so that the consultants shift some of their time and resources toward proposing a better work flow in the context of obtaining the best new system, sacrificing attention to some of the detail in the initially envisioned project?

The quality of the relationship with the client affects the degree to which such course corrections can be taken. My experience indicates that clients are delighted to have the opportunity. Should you encounter a situation where there is resistance, it could be a consideration to state in the deliverables that you pointed out an opportunity: "Investigations done in the course of determining functional requirements revealed challenges in the form of bottlenecks creating backlogs and in the form of duplicated procedures. The client chose not to address those challenges further at this time." (Naturally, we leave the door open to addressing the challenges in the future.)

THE FINAL DELIVERY

Whether the final delivery entails drawings, spreadsheets, workshops, budgets, purchase and licensing plans, marketing plans, or strategic plans, consultants at some point face the delivery dilemma. Do we show the client a draft or rough sketch early on for comment? Or do we polish every comma for the deadline? Once again, the relationship with the client shows the way. "Susan, here is an early draft—your input appreciated" can lead to key revisions (as in "The CEO would never accept recommendation 3. Is there a way to recast it?").

Ideally, in my experience, the final deliverable should be available to the client well before the deadline so that it can be tweaked in consideration of any optics and politics in play. The deliverable is sometimes the client's tool for advocating an approach; hence we must make sure our deliverable enables the purpose.

Where possible, look for an opportunity to discuss in person the final deliverable with the relevant stakeholder group. The main goal of a face-to-face discussion is to allow for questions and clarifications and to open the door for a consideration of possible next steps.

Typically, delivery is accompanied by a sense of anticipation on the part of the consultant; it is rewarding when the client is delighted with our work, and even more gratifying when concrete change takes place as a result of it. But we should not be surprised if our "product" isn't acted on or otherwise used. Not all organizations are ready to act beyond the step of seeking the advice of a consultant. We must "cash the check and move on."

BILLING AND GETTING PAID

Assuming everything proceeds without major disruption, you issue invoices matching the agreed-upon billing schedule. It is prudent to obtain confirmation that they have been received and sent into the payables process—you will regret not doing so if after 40 days it turns out your invoice was lost in transit.

My personal experience is that serious payment delays are rare. Should one occur, there could be many reasons. The natural progression would go from a polite inquiry at 35 days to a concerned follow-up at 45 days to a more directly worded communication at 60 days. With reasonably credible client assurances (an extended medical leave in accounts payable), we should probably wait 90 days before getting our lawyer involved to help. It is a reality that, if the client is experiencing a financial difficulty, consultants are the last to be paid. For that reason, it can't hurt to request a project initiation fee of 15–25 percent (knowing, of course, that such a fee may not be feasible for some organizations).

Postscript

Go for It—with Passion!

The practical tips offered in this primer are intended to help raise awareness of potential challenges so as to enable preparedness—not to paint a picture that consulting is only for the brave. Consulting is a most rewarding lifestyle, offering a great deal of excitement and satisfaction for those not afraid to give it their all. Just consider these typical statements:

> "It's true I work all the time—but half the time it doesn't feel like work because it is such a pleasure to be part of a success story for the client."

> "I treasure the friendships and professional networks that resulted from my projects."

> "Every day offers new opportunities to observe how differently people approach their challenges—and for me to become more perceptive. I grow professionally and personally with every new project."

> "I would never have known I had it in me—it is such a thrill to discover how much I really can contribute to making my clients succeed."

> "Sure, there were times I wondered what I'd been smoking when I decided to venture into consulting. But my only regret now is that I didn't do it sooner."

To everyone who may be pondering the possibility: you owe it to yourself to go for it!

Index

T

tact and delicacy, 89
target market, 48, 51
tax concerns
    and business structure, 53–54
    deductions, 56–57
    of self-employment, 28
taxes to be collected in contract, 79
technical services as service, 12
telephone services, 60
time commitment of consulting, 5
time line
    in contracts, 79
    in proposal, 71
time management skills, 35–36
trade shows, 60
training as service, 16
travel expenses, 41, 57, 76–77
trends
    assessment of, 19–22
    in libraries, 17–19
    market research in, 48
    in nonlibrary entities, 19
trust building, 38–39

U

uncommitted time, 36
upselling in proposals, 70
U.S. Small Business Administration, 52

V

vision statement, 52
volunteering, 64

W

web services for market research, 21
websites and web presence
    on business cards, 55
    as marketing, 67–68
    web resources for, 61
websites for the self-employed, 53, 60–62
word-of-mouth advertising, 66
work experience, 42–43
work steps in proposal, 71
working alone, comfort with, 35

Ulla de Stricker, founder and president of Toronto-based Ulla de Stricker and Associates, brings three decades of experience to bear on her clients' projects. Before she took the plunge into consulting in 1992, de Stricker held senior information industry positions with responsibility in various aspects of client relations and business strategy. During the 1980s she managed Canadian operations for Dialog Information Services; in the early 1990s she created a new electronic publishing unit and directed the market introduction of legal and tax-related products for Carswell/Thomson Professional Publishing. De Stricker speaks frequently at conferences internationally and contributes regularly to information industry journals. She holds an MA and MLS from McGill University, Montreal.